Mel Bay Presents

A Dossan of

Irish traditional music from Packie Manus Byrne of Donegal for tinwhistle, fiddle or flute

Compiled and edited by Jean Duval and Stephen Jones

85 jigs, highlands, airs, hornpipes and germans, reels, slip jigs, marches and polkas, mazurkas and waltzes

CD Contents

| 1 | Captain Taylor's march (#38, p.80) — [1:36]
| 2 | Showers of autumn (#15, p.48) & A dossan of heather (#9, p.40) — [2:13]
| 3 | The forgotten highland (#44, p.88) & Unnamed highland (#55, p.103) — [2:15]
| 4 | *An fear dall* (#24, p.61) — [1:49]
| 5 | The Glen Finn lass (#83, p.146) — [2:16]
| 6 | The tatty hokers (hornpipe) (#68, p.122); Blow the bellows (#61, p.112) & The three stars (#64, p.117) — [4:10]
| 7 | *An cailín rua* (The red-haired girl) (#28, p.67) — [1:24]
| 8 | Home from France (*Sa bhaile ó'n Fhrainc*) (#74, p.130) & The dangers of men (#77, p.134) — [2:35]
| 9 | *Mín a'Churráin* (#45, p.89) & Piddling Peggy (#42, p.86) — [2:11]
| 10 | Foyne's legacy (#16, p.50) & Away and over (#17, p.51) — [2:12]
| 11 | I'll marry you when me garden grows (#18, p.52) — [0:44]
| 12 | The schoolmaster's sister (#70, p.125) — [2:28]
| 13 | Lilting Ann (#54, p.102) — [0:58]
| 14 | *An bothán* (The little turf house) (#79, p.140) — [3:13]
| 15 | Piddling Peggy (#29, p.68)[2:01]
| 16 | Stepping stones (#5, p.34) & McShane's rambles (#2, p.28) — [2:24]
| 17 | The ghost's welcome (#59, p.108) — [2:02]
| 18 | The last star (#50, p.96) — [1:15]
| 19 | The storm (#3, p.30) & Teelin rowdies (#10, p.42) — [2:59]
| 20 | A Gweedore highland (#43, p.87); *An t-altán buí* (The yellow-faced rock) (#51, p.98) & Weans in skirts (#57, p.105) — [2:25]
| 21 | Forgetting the lesson (#1, p.26) — [3:28]
| 22 | *Ar thaobh na Carraige* (By the side of the rock) (#85, p.149) — [3:10]

Performers:
Jean Duval - whistle, flute, harmonica
Stephen Jones - whistle, low whistle, fiddle, bodhran, vocals
Johanne St. Laurent - harp
Lynda Dowker - keyboards
Reinhard Görner - guitar

MEL BAY®

© 2000 BY MEL BAY PUBLICATIONS, INC., PACIFIC, MO 63069.
ALL RIGHTS RESERVED. INTERNATIONAL COPYRIGHT SECURED. B.M.I. MADE AND PRINTED IN U.S.A.
No part of this publication may be reproduced in whole or in part, or stored in a retrieval system, or transmitted in any form or by any means, electronic, mechanical, photocopy, recording, or otherwise, without written permission of the publisher.

Visit us on the Web at www.melbay.com — E-mail us at email@melbay.com

A dossan of heather

A "dossan" is a large sprig or tuft of heather or hair. See p. 41.

Contributors

Jean Duval transcribed and edited the music from recordings made by Sharon & Richard Creasey, Packie Manus Byrne, Stephen Jones, and Reinhard Goerner

Stephen Jones transcribed Packie Manus' words and wrote the introduction and editorial text

Tomás Ó Canainn and **Liam Ó Cuinneagáin** acted as consultants for Irish orthography and usage

Lynda Dowker made the drawings from photographs by **Reinhard Goerner**

Christine Fortin typeset the music

Amélie Binette designed and set the type and laid out the pages

Photo credits

Sharon Creasy, p.144; Reinhard Goerner, pp.18,55;
Stephen Jones, pp.18,33,43,57,69,81,89,95,111,115,131,133,135;
Bob Naylor, pp.15,120; Brian Shuel, pp.31,72; Keith Wincoll, p.106.

Copyright of tunes

Many of the tunes in this collection are compositions by Packie Manus Byrne. He wishes to consign them all to the public domain. Musicians who perform or record any of these pieces are kindly asked to credit Packie, and mention the collection. In this way they will help these tunes to reach the widest possible audience, which is all Packie wants for them.

Other books by Packie Manus Byrne

Recollections of a Donegal Man. Roger Millington, 1989. ISBN 0 9514764 0 8

My Friend Flanagan: tall tales told by Packie Manus Byrne. Roger Millington, 1996. ISBN 0 9514764 1 6

Recordings by Packie Manus Byrne

Packie Byrne. EFDSS LP 1009. 1969.
Packie Manus Byrne: Songs of a Donegal Man. Topic Records 12TS257. 1975.
The Half Door. (With Bonnie Shaljean.) Dingle's Records DIN 302. 1977.
Roundtower. (With Bonnie Shaljean.) Dingle's Records DIN 311. 1981.
From Donegal and Back! Veteran VT132. 1995.

The following compilation albums each feature two songs by Packie:
Singing Men of Ulster. Innisfree/Green Linnet Records SIF 1005. 1977.
In the Smoke. (Packie's songs from *Songs of a Donegal Man*.) Globestyle CBORBD 088. 1996.

About this book

The tunes in this collection all come from one very unusual man: the much-loved singer, musician and storyteller **Packie Manus Byrne**.

Packie comes from Donegal in the northwest of Ireland – a region whose rich musical tradition has come to prominence in recent years through the work of such artists as Altan, Clannad and Enya.

Packie's stories will bring this tradition to life, giving you fascinating glimpses into the remote community where he grew up.

Catchy and tuneful, these pieces are suitable for **tin whistle, flute, uilleann pipes, fiddle, mandolin, banjo, accordion, concertina or any other traditional instrument**. Many are also ideal for the traditional art of lilting (the singing of dance tunes).

Whether you are a relative beginner or an expert traditional player, you'll find plenty to enjoy in this very special collection of Irish music!

Contents

Introduction		7
	Sources of the music and types of tunes	8
	A story for every tune	9
	The cast of musical characters	10
	How the collection was compiled	12
	Characteristic features of the tunes	13
	Packie's whistle style	16
Acknowledgments		21
A note on the Irish orthography used in this book		22
Notes on the transcriptions		23
	Guide to the speed of dance tunes	24
Jigs		25
	1. Forgetting the lesson	26
	2. McShane's rambles	28
	3. The storm	30
	4. The dark girl dressed in blue	32
	5. Stepping stones	34
	6. The Byrnes of Gleann Cholm Cille	36
	7. Merry hours of gladness	37
	8. Crossing the Oily river	38
	9. A dossan of heather	40
	10. Teelin rowdies	42
	11. The sheigh o' rye	44
	12. The sapper	45

13.	The lazy wife	46
14.	Willie dear	47
15.	Showers of autumn	48
16.	Foyne's legacy	50
17.	Away and over	51
18.	I'll marry you when me garden grows	52
19.	The peeler and the goat	53
20.	Socks on the crane	54
21.	The wheels of the train	56
22.	The half door	58
23.	*An t-éan sa chrann*	60
24.	*An fear dall*	61
25.	The buckasheen landy	62
26.	The collier laddie	64
27.	Paddy Bhillí *na rópaí*	65

Slip jigs — 66

28.	*An cailín rua* (The red-haired girl)	67
29.	Piddling Peggy	68
30.	The dawn pack	70
31.	Humours of whiskey	71

Marches and polkas — 72

32.	The Tummel march	73
33.	The fumbling chorister (march)	74
34.	A besom of heather (polka)	75
35.	The belling march	76
36.	I've got a bonnet (polka)	78
37.	*Mín na hÉireann* (march)	79
38.	Captain Taylor's march	80
39.	The swamp reed march	82
40.	The gap of Glenshane (march)	83
41.	The Fernden polka	84

Highlands — 85

42.	Piddling Peggy	86
43.	A Gweedore highland	87
44.	The forgotten highland	88
45.	*Mín a'Churráin*	89
46.	The crow's claw (Johnny Haughey's highland)	90
47.	Welcome home Rosie	91
48.	*An fharraige chiúin* (The calm sea)	92
49.	*An* highland *fada* (The long highland)	94
50.	The last star	96

51.	*An t-altán buí* (The yellow-faced rock)	98
52.	We're having a drop	99
53.	Behind the ditch in the garden	100
54.	Lilting Ann	102
55.	Unnamed highland	103
56.	The Willighan bush	104
57.	Weans in skirts	105

Reels — 106

58.	The dark girl dressed in blue	107
59.	The ghost's welcome	108
60.	Call the horse!	110
61.	Blow the bellows	112
62.	*An coileán cú*	114
63.	*An bata tí* (The house stick)	116
64.	The three stars	117

Hornpipes and germans — 118

65.	Unnamed german	119
66.	The Bonnie hop (german)	120
67.	The stuttering auctioneer (hornpipe)	121
68.	The tatty hokers (hornpipe)	122
69.	Barefoot Biddy (hornpipe)	124
70.	The schoolmaster's sister	125

Mazurkas and waltzes — 126

71.	Father Murphy's topcoat (Shoe the donkey)	127
72.	Alla Pio	128
73.	Rosie's *brachán* (mazurka)	129
74.	Home from France (*Sa bhaile ó'n Fhrainc*)	130
75.	Unnamed mazurka 1	132
76.	Unnamed mazurka 2	133
77.	The dangers of men	134

Airs — 135

78.	*Suan cloch teineadh* (The firestone lullaby)	136
79.	*An bothán* (The little turf house)	140
80.	The true lovers' discussion	141
81.	The barley field (air and hornpipe)	142
82.	The spinning wheel	145
83.	The Glen Finn lass	146
84.	A Welsh chapel hymn	147
85.	*Ar thaobh na Carraige* (By the side of the rock)	149

Index — 150

Packie Manus Byrne in the early 1970s. By courtesy of Packie Manus Byrne.

Introduction

Packie Manus Byrne is a man of many parts. The list of his talents—traditional singer, whistle player, actor, storyteller, comedian—gives some idea of why he has been called "a living cultural treasure." To understand the other reasons, you will have to meet him, drink tea with him, discuss life, people and music with him, and enjoy his poetic language, his irresistible sense of fun, and his bottomless fund of stories—funny and sad, true and false, but all fascinating.

Here, however, is a chance to get to know Packie Manus through music. Gathered here are the tunes he loves best, and the ones that he is most anxious to pass on to future generations of traditional musicians.

Perhaps the most remarkable thing about this collection—apart from the beauty of the music—is that it is, in essence, a time capsule: it is composed mostly of tunes that were played in a remote townland of southwest Donegal between 1925 and 1937, when Packie first left home; many of them have rarely been heard since.

The townland into which Packie was born in 1917 was Corkermore, a few miles inland from the towns of Killybegs and Ardara. Many homes, including that of Packie's parents, were "rambling houses" in which neighbours and visitors would gather for nights of song, dance, and talk—three activities in which Packie began to show an almost obsessive interest very early on:

> 'Before I went to school, I was four or five, I used to be learning songs and tunes and things, and everyone that could would get a clout at me because I was a nuisance. I would be shouting my head off when the old people wanted to get chatting amongst themselves, and I would be put out into the field; I could sing my heart out in the field, they wouldn't have me in the house at all.'

Packie's career as a public performer began very soon after: he remembers singing at a school concert aged five, wearing a green knitted suit—cardigan and knickers—made by his mother. The young artiste was rewarded with half a crown, a princely sum that may have helped to convince him that music was the path he should follow in life. By the time he was ten Packie had begun to accompany his parents to hooleys and weddings. Although he could play whistle quite well at this age, singing was what was expected of him on these occasions.

Formal education finished for Packie at age fourteen, and he spent the next few years helping his father and elder brother on the family farm. He also began droving cattle, an occupation to which he returned some years later. Packie's claim that he got much more of an education droving than he did at school should not be taken as a slight upon his schoolmaster (for Packie's grasp of the three Rs would shame many a university entrant of today), but rather as a clue to the rich experiences that this occupation brought him. Tramping the roads of Donegal and the neighbouring counties, Packie learned to deal with people and situations of every kind. He also got plenty of opportunities to play music. Many of his compositions came to him while droving, and although he usually carried a whistle, he most often made the tunes by lilting them as he walked.

In 1937 Packie left home to seek work in the industrial Midlands of England. He recalls that his singing was appreciated in boarding houses, although he would generally have to wait until nobody was in the house before he felt free to play the whistle. Within a very short time, however, he was moving away from traditional music, playing saxophone in dance bands and singing in variety shows. After a few years he began to shuttle back and forth between England, where he worked in an astonishing variety of jobs, and Ireland, where he returned to farming and droving, and occasionally engaged in a less respectable occupation: smuggling cattle and tea across the Northern Ireland border![1]

By the 1950s, the musical life of rural Donegal had changed dramatically. What Packie calls "cowboy songs" were all the rage. Country-house dancing was dead, and in halls around the county the old sets, mazurkas and highlands had all but completely given way to foxtrots and waltzes. But, defying the vagaries of fashion and Packie's long estrangement from traditional music, the old songs and tunes began to bubble back to the surface of his mind. He spent several years in hospital in Ireland recovering from tuberculosis. Several decades before music therapy was invented, Packie's doctors realized that encouraging him to play and sing would help him to full recovery. He started attending *fleánna ceoil* (traditional-music festivals), taking first place in the ballad-singing competition on a number of occasions.

In 1964 Packie was invited to perform at a folk festival at Cecil Sharp House in London, substituting for the famous Donegal fiddler John Doherty (John having gone walkabout, apparently quailing before the prospect of sea travel). This was the dawn of the folk revival in England, and after his appearance at the festival Packie's future as a folk performer was assured. He continued to play at clubs and festivals all over Britain until the late 1980s.

Sources of the music and types of tunes

I began by saying that this collection can be seen as a time capsule, for it contains many otherwise forgotten gems perfectly preserved in the amber of Packie's memory. Packie is one of the last survivors of the last generation of traditional musicians to learn his music in a purely oral tradition. He was in his teens by the time neighbours returned from America with wind-up gramophones and records, and he was a grown man before there was a radio in his parents' house. He has never learned to read music, but has relied on a razor-sharp musical memory, honed to the point where he could memorize a lengthy ballad after two or three hearings, and even tunes that he heard played only once. His powers of recall are the reason we have been able to assemble this body of music.

Packie has remained strongly attached to the music of his youth. He has often remarked that while he was growing up, the tunes and songs "were in the air" around him; it was inevitable that they should strike deep roots in such a sensitive musical nature as Packie's. Just as he has never lost his accent, he has never broken with the musical tradition of his home townland. Perhaps it is his way of keeping alive his fond memories of the stimulating folk culture that flourished so strongly when he was a boy, and which all had but vanished within a few years of his leaving home.

Unlike many Irish musicians who lived long years in England, Packie spent little time in the fertile pub-session scene, and was therefore less influenced by players from other parts of Ireland. His most "Irish" period in England was in the Manchester of the 1960s, where he mixed with musicians of the calibre of Des Donnelly (the famous fiddler from County

---

1. Packie's adventurous life is chronicled in his autobiography, **Recollections of a Donegal Man,** ed. Stephen Jones (Roger Millington, 1989). Readers will also find in its pages a good deal of information about musical life in Packie's home townland.

Tyrone), played as a duo in clubs with the travelling piper Felix Doran (brother of the more celebrated Johnny), and stayed in the same house as the great Séamus Ennis. Yet it seems Packie felt less at home in the Irish pubs than he did in folk clubs, where it gave him "great satisfaction that a dozen or so people could sit together and sing the old songs." He loved the camaraderie and self-help of the early folk movement, and enjoyed finding an appreciative audience not only for his vast store of traditional ballads but also for his prodigious gift for comedy and every class of nonsense.[2] His relative isolation from the Irish pub scene undoubtedly helped to keep his repertoire of traditional tunes largely undiluted.

Many of the tunes presented here Packie learned from members of his family or from neighbours and visitors. A number were simply tunes being played for dancing in the local area, and beyond that he knows nothing of their origins. Others were tunes of songs, or were made from song tunes (Packie himself being the chief artisan of these transformations). Many tunes Packie knows to be of Scottish origin; often, these were brought back to Donegal from Scotland by migratory workers (known as "tatty hokers"[3]). At least fourteen of the tunes are Packie's own compositions, on top of the half-dozen that he made out of existing song tunes (and even, in one case, a hymn!).

The proportions of different types of tunes in the collection reflect Packie's musical tastes, with the exception of slow airs, of which he is especially fond: with only eight examples, they are distinctly under-represented here.[4] Slow airs aside, Packie has a pronounced fondness for jigs, which make up a third of the collection with 27 examples. Highlands are also great favourites of his, and 16 of these archetypally Donegal tunes comprise about one fifth of the pieces presented here. The remainder is made up of seven reels, ten marches and polkas, four slip jigs, six hornpipes and "germans"[5], and seven mazurkas and miscellaneous oddities. The relative paucity of reels, running counter to the modern trend for these tunes to squeeze all other kinds out of every session and out of almost every collection, is no accident. Packie regrets their overarching dominance. Those who are tempted to take exception to this point of view can instead take heart in the fact that almost all the highlands, doubled, straightened out and speeded up a bit, make fine reels. The rest of us will take delight in the melodiousness of the jigs and the stark beauty of the highlands played as highlands.

A story for every tune

In most collections of traditional music, all that is presented of a tune is the bare skeleton of notes on the stave and perhaps a name. Even names are often lost in the oral-transmission process, particularly in the pub or festival session, where so many tunes are learned either

---

2. Connoisseurs of humour are referred to **My Friend Flanagan: tall tales told by Packie Manus Byrne** (Roger Millington, 1996) for a sample of Packie's storytelling talents

3. "Potato lifters". See the text accompanying no. 68.

4. This is chiefly because many of the airs which Packie often plays can be found in substantially the same settings in other collections (a number of those that we might have included are in Tomás Ó Canainn's collection, **Traditional Slow Airs of Ireland**, Ossian 1995). A further disincentive to expanding our somewhat parsimonious selection of airs lay in the notorious difficulty of satisfactorily transcribing Irish slow airs, especially as regards fitting them into a time signature, and the fact that they are almost equally difficult to interpret properly from the transcribed versions.

5. Also known as "German barn dances", these tunes are very similar to hornpipes as far as speed and form are concerned.

The only known photograph of Packie Manus' parents, Connell and Maria Byrne, probably taken in the 1920s. By courtesy of Packie Manus Byrne.

on the spot or later, through tape recordings. All this makes it easy to forget that every tune originated with a particular player in a particular community, and had its own significance and associations, its own story.

> 'Some of the older folks had a little story attached to every tune they played. If it was an air, they'd tell you the bones of the story. If it was a jig, if there wasn't really a story behind it, they could tell you who used to dance to it. "Mary so-and-so wouldn't dance to any other tune than this one," because it was her favourite tune. They all had little stories attached to them, and the thing about it is, a hell of a lot of the stories were true.'

We have endeavoured to remain faithful to this tradition. Packie is now, of course, one of the "older folks" and, with his keen memory and gift for storytelling, has indeed a story for almost every tune. Where he does not, we have given whatever relevant information he could provide.

The cast of musical characters

The names of the neighbours and family members from whom Packie learned tunes keep cropping up in the stories. A brief introduction to the most significant of these musical influences seems appropriate here.

Fiddler John Gallagher of Ardara, holding a "tin fiddle". These remarkable instruments, made of sheet steel by tinsmiths, were quite common in Donegal in the early part of the 20th century. This very fine example was made by Mickey Doherty, the father of two giants of Donegal fiddle music, John and Mickey Doherty. Photo: Stephen Jones.

Although he did not play an instrument, Packie's father, Connell Byrne, was a keen lilter and storyteller. Packie's mother Maria (née Gallagher) also sang and lilted continually. Packie's grand-uncle "Big Pat" Byrne, a formidable fiddler and a formidable man, is one of the most important sources of tunes. Pat's sister Ann Byrne lived with her brother and has a tune named after her (**Lilting Ann**, no. 54).

Both of Packie's sisters, Ann and Memie, married men called Patrick Keeney. Ann's husband was a fine fiddle player. Two women named Bridget Sweeney were important figures in Packie's musical experience. The first, "Big Bridget" Sweeney (née Gallagher), was Packie's mother's aunt. The second was Biddy Sweeney of Corkermore. Both these women were noted singers and lilters.[6]

Paddy Boyle, also known as Paddy Bhillí *na rópaí*, was a well-known fiddle player from Calhame, a townland near Killybegs. He was frequently invited to play at "big nights" (house dances) all over southwest Donegal.

Other influences were John Haughey, a fiddler from the townland of Gleann Baile Dubh; John Byrne (no relation), a fiddler from Ballywogs; Pat Kennedy, a melodeon player from Dunkineely; fiddler John Gallagher of Ardara and his father Paddy; and the Campbells from Silverhill, Glenties.

---

6. More detailed portraits of these members of Packie's family and other musicians are to be found in **Recollections of a Donegal Man**.

Another musician whose name occurs a number of times is Bonnie Shaljean. Packie came into contact with her, not in the Donegal of the 1920s, but on the London folk scene of the 1970s. Bonnie was a young American harpist and singer with whom Packie formed a duo to perform in clubs and at festivals. They played together for about ten years from the mid-1970s on and made two LP records for Dingle's Records. One of the tunes in the collection (no. 66) has been named after Bonnie. She now lives in Cork City, where she plays and teaches Irish music on harp and keyboards.

How the collection was compiled

Perhaps the first person to realize the value of Packie's tunes was Sharon Creasey, a flute player who during the 1980s lived not far from Packie in north London. It was through Sharon that I got to know Packie better, and I suggested to her that she should assemble and publish a collection of Packie's music. This plan was shelved in favour of Sharon's idea that I should help Packie to compile his autobiography, RECOLLECTIONS OF A DONEGAL MAN.

In the process of tape-recording Packie's words for his story, I also taped several hours of talk and tunes, with the idea that the tune-book would form the next project. A very valuable tape of material had already been made by Sharon and her husband Richard. Packie also supplied me with various home recordings of his playing made over the years by himself or others, some dating from the 1960s. RECOLLECTIONS OF A DONEGAL MAN was published in 1989, but by that time I had moved to Canada, and by 1996 the tapes had been sitting in a box for ten years.

The job of compiling the collection was finally set in motion thanks to the skills, enthusiasm and determination of my friend and musical colleague Jean Duval—another flute and whis-

Stephen Jones, Packie Manus and Sharon Creasey playing at Packie's 70th birthday party at the Northumberland Arms, Goodge Street, London, February 18, 1987.

tle player. Realizing that, if left to me, the tapes might easily sit undisturbed for another decade, Jean[7] volunteered to assemble the collection by transcribing the tunes on these tapes and on Packie's published recordings, on the condition that I take care of the accompanying text. He set about the work of transcription with painstaking care and accuracy. This was a very considerable job, since the quality of the home recordings was often poor, and many tunes appeared in multiple, subtly differing versions. Jean, who had initially thought the collection might make 15 or 20 pieces, never showed a sign of discouragement as tape after tape was unearthed and the quantity of work multiplied.

By the end of 1996, about 80 pieces had been committed to paper, and Jean felt he had done all he could without Packie's input. So in February 1997 we spent a week with Packie Manus in Ardara, where he has lived since moving back to Donegal from London in 1987. Jean (who by this time had developed an uncanny ability to play whistle in Packie's own style) played all his transcriptions to Packie, asking him to approve each piece, and to clear up ambiguities and select the most authentic version where necessary.

We took this opportunity to question Packie more closely about the sources of each tune, which produced a wealth of information and stories, given in the pages of the collection alongside the relevant piece. The visit also stirred Packie's musical memory, and a further half-dozen tunes were added to the collection. Since many of the pieces, especially the highlands and reels, had no names, we enlisted Packie's help and creativity in the enjoyable task of inventing relevant titles for unnamed tunes. Packie was pleased with the results, since he likes tunes to have proper names.

This collection, then, is very much a joint effort between Packie Manus, Jean Duval and myself, building on early work done by Sharon Creasey. All the musical transcription was done by Jean, while the transcription of Packie's words fell to me. The rest of the text is by me, with input from Jean, especially in the sections of the Introduction dealing with the characteristic features of the tunes and with Packie's whistle style, which draw on notes that Jean made during the transcription process. All the material and all the inspiration comes from Packie Manus, whose own words make up the bulk of the comments about the individual tunes.

The remainder of this introductory section contains a more technical discussion of the tunes and of Packie's whistle style. Readers who find their eyes glazing over as they read on are invited to get out their instrument and skip to the tunes and accompanying stories!

Characteristic features of the tunes

Players who explore this collection will soon come to appreciate the unique character of Packie's tunes. They are simple and yet very alluring. Many have a distinctly Donegal flavour, and nearly all have an ancient ring about them.

An immediately striking feature is the limited range of the melodies. Exactly two thirds of the tunes go no higher than f♯'. Of the remaining third, two tunes reach d" and six b' (the most common top note in Irish dance music). About 20 per cent of the tunes have a range of only one octave and another 15 per cent one octave and one note (d - e').

---

7. Jean, a native of Quebec, wishes English-speakers to be aware that the pronunciation of his name is much closer to "Seán" than to "Gene"!

This restricted range is almost certainly due to the fact that these tunes were frequently lilted, and Packie's comments reveal that, despite the large number of fiddlers in the area, the music for impromptu dancing sessions was very often provided by a lilter. As noted above, many of the tunes were originally songs, but the fact that the turn, or second part of the tune, keeps within the first octave plus one or two notes reinforces the idea that these pieces were lilted after their conversion into dance tunes. Packie's own compositions keep within the same boundaries, for the same reasons, as his comment about the reel **Blow the bellows** (no. 61), makes clear: "That's another one-octave one. Makes them easier to sing!"[8]

As far as the modes and scales used in the tunes are concerned, Packie has an obvious preference for the whistle's natural scales, which are (on a D whistle) D major and E dorian ("E minor" with a major 6th), but he also plays in G major, the C natural being obtained either by half-holing or using "forked" fingering.[9]

D major, E dorian and G major respectively account for 43, 25 and 14 per cent of Packie's repertoire. D myxolydian, the scale of the highland bagpipes (major with a minor 7th) accounts for only 8 per cent[10], although three tunes alternate between D myxolydian and D major. We have never heard Packie play in the Aeolian mode (minor scale with a minor sixth), except for the **Welsh chapel hymn** (no. 84), which is apparently of "foreign" origin.

Gapped scales, either penta- or hexatonic, occur in slightly over one third of Packie's tunes. We have a real rarity in **The swamp reed march**, no. 39, a tune that is missing three notes and can thus be classed as tetratonic! (It may be also the only tune in the whistle repertoire that can be performed by a one-handed player...)

The absence of the third degree ("neutral" tunes, with no third to lend them a definite major or minor cast) occurs frequently in jigs (e.g., nos. 5 and 14-18) and highlands (nos. 49-51, 54 and 55), and in nos. 30 and 37. It is interesting to note that tunes with the third and sixth degrees missing can be easily played in either D or E on the whistle: an example is **Stepping stones**, no. 5.

Another characteristic of Packie's music, and one that reflects his experimental turn of mind, is a marked fluidity of form. He greatly enjoys adapting tunes, making airs out of hornpipes, and jigs out of reels. While this is common enough in Irish music in general[11], Packie has taken this practice of "trans-forming" tunes further than any other traditional musician that we know of. Good examples are the tune **Piddlin' Peggy**, a Packie Manus composition which he plays as a slip jig (no. 29) or a highland (no. 42), and which also makes an excel-

---

8. Tunes with similarly limited ranges are quite common in the repertoire of Donegal fiddlers, making them suitable for being played by two or more fiddlers in octaves, a frequent practice in that county.

9. Although Packie habitually plays tunes in D major and E dorian, he can instantly transpose them into G major and A dorian. At times we have played Packie's tunes in other keys and he has joined in without apparently noticing the change. (This has convinced us that he plays entirely by ear, without relying on "finger memory".)

10. This suggests that, as far as Packie's repertoire is concerned, the influence of the highland bagpipes cannot be advanced to explain the limited range of the tunes. Some of Packie's tunes, particularly highlands and jigs, seem to us to be more closely related to existing Scottish tunes than could be explained by coincidence. In these cases, it seems that the fiddle—the prime instrument for dance music in Donegal—has had more importance than the pipes.

11. And in Donegal in particular: as Packie points out, many highlands were slowed-down reels, or were derived from Scottish strathspeys, this time speeded up and with "some of the kinks ironed out of them".

Packie Manus in the late 1970s. Photo: Bob Naylor.

lent reel; ***Mín a'Churráin*** (no. 45), a highland which Packie also plays as an air and a march (see ***Mín na hÉireann***, no. 37); and ***The dark girl dressed in blue***, which he plays as a jig (no. 4), a reel (no. 58) and a barn dance. The most common transformation, however, is Packie's habit of making an air out of a dance tune and playing the two together (***Captain Taylor***, no. 38, ***The half door***, no. 22).

Packie's whistle style

The whistle is Packie's main instrument, and his playing of it is unique. A discussion of his style, apart from being interesting for its own sake, may help to shed light on the transcriptions and suggest ways of approaching these tunes to players less familiar with Donegal music.

In general, Packie is reluctant to enter into discussions of his whistle style. This is certainly partly due to modesty, but it may also owe something to the fact that in the Donegal of his youth the whistle was not taken seriously as an instrument for dancing to.

> 'Whistles were toys, they were for children. The day I was born there were whistles about the house, because my mother used to play the whistle a little. There was the old tapered one with the bit of timber in the mouthpiece, and 'twould lie up maybe for a year or so, and 'twouldn't be dried before it would be left lying up, and it would be red with rust, and the taste would be something shocking off it!
>
> The first whistle I ever remember being my own, a fellow called Francie McGinley bought it for me. Now there was a christening somewhere, and Francie was a godfather to some youngster. At that time you had to take the youngsters all the way into Killybegs to get them christened, and there was a house in Killybegs, a shop called Quigley's, and it was the only place in this end of the county that you could get whistles. So he bought me a whistle and it cost one penny, and they were known as penny whistles at that time, which was another reason why they weren't regarded as very valuable.
>
> My uncle Patrick Gallagher, my mother's brother, was a good whistler. I think he used to play for dancing, but there was always so many fiddle players around that nobody bothered with flutes or whistles or anything for dancing. All dancing was done to fiddle music. Fiddle was number one around here, and in fact it still is.
>
> Did I play these tunes for dancing on the whistle? I might, you know, in my younger days, when there would be no fiddler available and no lilter. Packie Manus would get a clout in the ear and "Pick up that whistle and play a tune for us!" You done it for self-preservation more than anything else.
>
> I don't know if I copied my uncle Patrick's style of playing the whistle. Maybe I did, unintentionally. I'm not sure about that.'

Wherever the inspiration for his style came from, Packie's phrasing is very musical, and has—as we might expect from such an accomplished singer—a distinctive singing quality. Unlike many traditional flute and whistle players, who use tonguing sparingly or not at all, Packie admirably demonstrates the expressive possibilities of this technique. In fact, he makes more generous use of tonguing than perhaps any other whistle player in Ireland.[12] There is a parallel to be made between Packie's employment of tonguing and the considerable use of single-stroke bowing by Donegal fiddlers.

Tongued triplets are a very noticeable characteristic of Packie's playing, occurring on the same note, or with the first note doubled and an adjacent note as the third component, and less frequently on three consecutive notes upward or downward. The parallel with fiddling is obvious here. The following transcription of the well-known reel *The skylark*, taken from his 1969 record PACKIE BYRNE, published by the English Folk Dance and Song Society, will demonstrate the extent to which Packie is able to lace his playing with expertly executed tongued triplets.

Reel The skylark, *showing Packie's use of tongued triplets.*

To produce the tongued triplets, which are beautifully clear and even, Packie uses a technique derived from lilting: his tongue makes a "diddle-dee" movement rather than the "ta-ka-ta" recommended in classical flute or recorder technique.

> 'Nearly everyone will do the twiddlies with their fingers. Now I used to, when the fingers were really nimble. I had very nimble fingers at one time. But then I discovered that to make any job of a reel like that

---

12. At least among members of his own generation. Some younger players, notably Seán Ryan in Galway, have developed a modern style making very extensive use of tonguing. As might be expected, Packie particularly admires this new style of playing.

Jean Duval transcribing from Packie Manus' playing, Ardara, February 1997. During an evening out, the tune Barefoot Biddy *had resurfaced in Packie's memory. Arriving home at 1am, Jean and Packie set to work immediately, Packie not waiting to take off his cap! Photo: Stephen Jones.*

Packie whistles as Jean transcribes, Ardara, Febuary 1997. Photo: Reinhard Goerner.

> [*The skylark*], I had to put in the little trebly things, and I done it with me tongue. Well now, anyone can do it if they practise. You'll do anything with practice you know. Practice makes master!
>
> I do it with the tongue against the top of my mouth, but I cannot do it so well since I got the false teeth. When I had my own teeth I had much more room for the tongue to hop about! Yi-till-diddly, i-till-diddly... You could keep that diddly-diddly thing going all the time.'

Packie will occasionally use tongued staccato at the end of a phrase or in particular sections of a dance tune to add expression or to suit a movement in the dance (**Piddlin' Peggy** slip jig, no. 29, **The sapper**, no. 12). The only tunes where Packie uses very little tonguing are marches. Perhaps this is in unconscious imitation of the highland pipes, or in order to create a flow that is more suitable for marching than for dancing to.

In Packie's view, many of the older generation of whistle players used tonguing quite frequently. In his own case, as he says above, he began to incorporate more tonguing into his playing when he began to lose agility in his fingers.[13] Arthritis has for decades severely restricted movement of the second and third fingers of his right hand (and has ultimately

---

13. Packie tells us that his experience as a dance-band saxophonist in the 1930s and 1940s helped him master his tonguing technique—surely one of the earliest instances of popular music influencing the performance of an Irish traditional player!

caused him to stop playing altogether). As a result, Packie uses finger ornamentation sparingly in most tunes. "Cuts" (single grace notes) are played on E, F♯, G, A and B (never on C or D). In highlands, cuts and triplets are used interchangeably. Packie uses trills extensively in slow airs, but occasionally (and unusually) on longer notes in dance tunes.

The roll, that characteristically Irish and now ubiquitous ornament, is a device that Packie does not care for. He feels that, as used by many players, rolls tend to obscure rather than highlight the melody:

> 'To be quite honest, I'm not too keen on this rolling business, because I reckon it takes the flavour out of the tune, especially for the listener. It sounds good, especially on a whistle or a flute, but [without it] a listener can pick up the tune much easier. Now that's only my opinion, but I know what I like to listen to. I think really it has to do with the way the notes form in the tune.'

Interestingly, Packie describes using a glottal stop in slow airs, a device favoured by *seán-nos* singers:

> 'On slow airs, you would do it from your throat, you would open and close your throat, with the back of your tongue, and cut off the note... [demonstrates].'

Breath control is an important aspect in the playing of any wind instrument. Fascinatingly, Packie taught himself the technique of circular breathing when still a youngster by blowing into a basin of water through a straw, practising until he could keep the flow of bubbles coming while he was breathing in. This was undoubtedly useful when playing the saxophone, but Packie apparently continued to rely partially on this technique when playing whistle, particularly after he had a lung removed as the result of tuberculosis.

Variation is a vital component of Irish traditional music, and Packie is an unconscious master of the art. However, he dislikes ostentatious, premeditated variations and deplores the habit of many showy players of making radical departures from the basic tune. The following passage, describing music played for a house dance, sums up his attitude:

> 'The highland would be one tune all the way through. Maybe there would be a change, but very seldom. My brother-in-law, Patrick Keeney, who was a great highland player, would never change. He would play the same highland through to the end of the dance—six or seven or maybe eight turns. People who weren't accustomed to this highland business would get very fed up listening to him, they would be waiting for some change, and there would be no change. The little decorations and variations did come in: Big Pat, and Francie Dearg, and Con Cassidy were great for that, and quite a lot of the old musicians. But they kept to the basic tune, they never went away off the tune altogether. It was the same thing again and again. And the dancing's the same. All the turns are identical.'

The "little decorations and variations" are very much a feature of Packie's own playing. While he does not try to impress the listener with endless invention, he rarely plays a tune the same way twice, adding variations that are simple but effective.

> 'I suppose there was no set way of playing them tunes, there was so many people whacking at them, and nobody took a blind bit o' notice whether there was trills or diddlies or anything put into them.'

In highlands, he generally starts with a basic statement of a tune, gradually adding more elaborate features (such as triplets—as, for example, in **An fharraige chiúin**, no. 48), or emphasizing key notes (as in **The last star**, no. 50) with each repetition of the tune.

Another form of variation is the use of different parts, especially in jigs. On our tape recordings, several jigs (e.g. **Willie dear**, no. 14) appear with two or three alternative second parts, or "turns", at different times. One of the highlands, **Behind the ditch in the garden**, no. 53, occurs with four different second parts. Packie's musicianship is such that, if he forgets a part of a tune, he can often improvise another that makes just as much musical sense as the original.[14]

Packie's musical abilities do not stop at singing and playing whistle. He is able to play a tune on almost any instrument, and on quite a few objects that would not ordinarily be classed as instruments! Apart from the whistle, he has played mouth organ, flute, saxophone, keyboards, and has experimented with the fiddle and the uillean pipes. As a boy, he would play tunes on whistles fashioned from reeds by his brother Jim (see **The swamp reed march**, no. 39), and can still whistle beautifully (i.e., with his mouth). Shortly after his eightieth birthday, he demonstrated to us his extraordinary ability to play a tune using only the mouthpiece of a recorder or whistle, forming the notes by cupping his fingers around the open end. His early club performances featured such oddities as tuned horseshoes strung on a wire to form a kind of glockenspiel, and a musical bicycle pump, played like a trombone, which had a three-octave range. His 1970s model "abluphone" was a complicated bagpipe-like creation comprised of whistles joined together with rubber shower tubing, and in the 1980s his "pandemonium" was a one-man bandstand based around an electronic keyboard and featuring hooters, cymbals and other sound effects.

Packie has often quoted a favourite saying of his father's, expressing admiration of a gifted musician: "He could take music out of a fresh loaf!" I am sure that Packie's father must frequently have aimed this phrase at—if he did not coin it for—his second son. I am equally confident that readers, after "listening" to the stories and trying out the tunes preserved in these pages, will not only acknowledge the remarkable talent but also enjoy the warm personality and irrepressible humour of our friend Packie Manus.

Stephen Jones, Montreal, October 1999

---

14. This fluidity of the turn was probably much more common in earlier times, before the days of printed collections and recordings: an amusing story is given in Brendan Breathnach's Folk Music and Dances of Ireland (Mercier Press, 1971). "The local priest, having dispersed the dancers at a crossroad gathering, asked the blind musician, with heavy sarcasm, whether he could play the *Our Father*. The musician replied that if his reverence would whistle the tune, he was sure he would be able to turn it for him."

Acknowledgments

We are deeply indebted to Sharon Creasey for realizing the value of Packie's music and stories and for passing his tunes on to us and to other musicians. Were it not for Sharon, neither Packie's autobiography nor this collection would have seen the light of day, and only the distance between Canada and Scotland prevented her from playing a greater role in the project. We also wish to thank another friend and musical colleague, Reinhard Goerner (better known as Golo) who accompanied us on our visit to Packie in 1997 and expertly recorded the entire week's proceedings in photographs and on tape. Lynda Dowker, Jean's neighbour in rural Quebec and another member of our musical coterie, provided the beautiful drawings. The devotion and technical expertise of Christine Fortin, who typeset the tunes, and Amélie Binette, who did the graphic design and page layout, is greatly appreciated.

We are grateful to Emily Andrews, Lee Cadieux, Kate Crossan, Isabeau Kinsella Doucet, Seán McCutcheon and Bill White for reading the manuscript and making helpful suggestions. We are indebted to Packie's old friend John Moulden for providing various pieces of information and the words to the song *Finn waterside*. Special thanks go to our Irish-language consultants, Liam Ó Cuinneagáin and Tomás Ó Canainn.

Our greatest gratitude, of course, goes to Packie Manus, for passing on to us these tunes that we love so much, and for giving us the enormous pleasure and privilege of working with him once again.

Stephen Jones and Jean Duval, Montreal, October 1999

It's nice to see people from far away places having so much interest in our traditional music, and it's also heartening to see so many young people playing Irish music. Thanks to them, the old music will not die. Sad to say, nearly all the musicians of my generation have passed on to a better land (may they all rest in peace), but with the vast number of young musicians taking up where the older ones left off, the future of our national music is well assured.

I would like to dedicate the music in this book both to Sharon Creasey, my very good friend, whose music, encouragement and introductions made this book and others possible, and to Bonnie Shaljean, who tolerated my eccentricities and kept me on the straight and narrow musical path for over a decade of working together in the world of folk music.

Bless ye all.

Packie Manus Byrne, Ardara, August 1998

A note on the Irish orthography used in this book

Packie Manus is not a native speaker of Irish, but grew up close to an Irish-speaking part of Donegal.

> 'There's a little stream before you go into Corkermore, and that was the border between the Gaeltacht and the English-speaking area. I was born on the far side of the stream and therefore I was not in the Gaeltacht, but Ardara was in the Gaeltacht. I understand quite a lot of Irish through listening to my father and my mother—my mother was from the Gaeltacht, from the mountains way out.'

Packie uses Irish words in the names of tunes in the collection and in some of the stories that accompany them. A number of these words are peculiar to western Donegal, and in many cases Packie's pronunciation and usage also appear to be native to his part of the country. Packie's spelling of these words is partly remembered and partly phonetic, and may or may not reflect the way they would have been written by a literate local Irish-speaker of his parents' generation. And, of course, Irish orthography has been reformed since Packie's schooldays.

All this presented a dilemma regarding the spelling of the Irish words used in this book. The only practical way of achieving accuracy and consistency seemed to be to conform to modern Irish spelling and usage. In this regard we wish to thank for their generous help Tomás Ó Canainn, who carefully combed through the text and provided us with the standard modern orthography, and Liam Ó Cuinneagáin of Oideas Gael,[15] who helped us with the spelling of various local and "problem" words and Donegal placenames. Any errors which may have crept in since their perusal of the manuscript are the editor's responsibility.

---

15. The Irish-language college and cultural centre in Gleann Cholm Cille (Glencolumbkille).

Notes on the transcriptions

Many of the tunes in the collection appear several times on the source tape recordings, and these versions differ to varying degrees—some only slightly, others quite radically. Where there were significantly different versions, I asked Packie to choose the variant he wanted to be given in the book. Although in some cases I have transcribed two or three playings of a tune to demonstrate Packie's use of variation, for the most part I have assembled a single version, sometimes combining variations or ornaments from more than one playing. In one respect—Packie's prolific use of triplets—some settings have been, if anything, simplified in the interests of legibility. All the transcriptions given here have been approved by Packie.

As mentioned in the introduction, Packie plays most of his tunes in either D major or E dorian. I have transcribed them as he played them, resisting the temptation to inject more variety into the collection by arbitrarily transposing some of the tunes into other keys common in Irish music—G or A major, or A dorian. However, readers are encouraged to play the tunes in whatever key best suits their instrument. Fiddle players in particular will find that many of the one-octave D major tunes will sound very well in A major, whereas players of flutes, whistles and pipes might like them better in G.

With one exception, I have not used dotted notation in the highlands, reels or hornpipes, despite the fact that Packie's playing of some tunes is particularly strongly accented (the exception is the slow hornpipe, **The schoolmaster's sister**, no. 70). As experienced players know, of course, neither dotted nor undotted notation accurately represents the rhythm traditional players use in these types of tunes, which in reality falls somewhere between the two.

The main forms of ornamentation used by Packie are represented as follows (for more information, see the section of the introduction dealing with Packie's whistle style):

The symbol + represents a **cut** (single grace note), and **tr** a **trill**. **Upward slides** are indicated by an inverted tie (slur) linking two notes.

Triplets are written without staccato dots. Obviously, where triplets occur on the same note, Packie plays them staccato, tonguing each component, but he also uses this technique (to great effect) on almost all occurrences of triplets spread over two or three adjacent notes.

As for tempo, the table below provides a guide to the speed at which Packie habitually plays these tunes.

Guide to the speed at which Packie plays dance tunes

Jigs	♩. = 110-130
Slip jigs	♩. = 115
Marches	♩ = 112-121
Polkas	♩ = > 123
Highlands	𝅗𝅥 = 83-90
Reels	𝅗𝅥 = 91-111
Hornpipes and germans	𝅗𝅥 = 85-95
Slow hornpipe	♩ = 105
Mazurkas and waltzes	𝅗𝅥 = 150-172

If readers have any information on the names and origins of any of the pieces in the collection, we would be delighted to hear from you. Please contact us via the publisher.

Jean Duval, Peveril, Quebec, October 1999

Jigs

'In our house, jigs were played for step dancing and for set dancing, ceili dancing, and the old Donegal set was nearly all jigs. In the old days the same tunes were played for a particular set in the dance. The old set around here, there was a different beat for each turn of the dance.

Jigs were danced quite a lot in the old days, but not as much as reels. Reels seemed to take over. And they still do. You sit down in a session today, and you'll have half-a-dozen reels to one jig. And it's a pity, because I think the jigs are lovely tunes. I play many more jigs than reels, because I love them. They have a kind of a swing to them.'

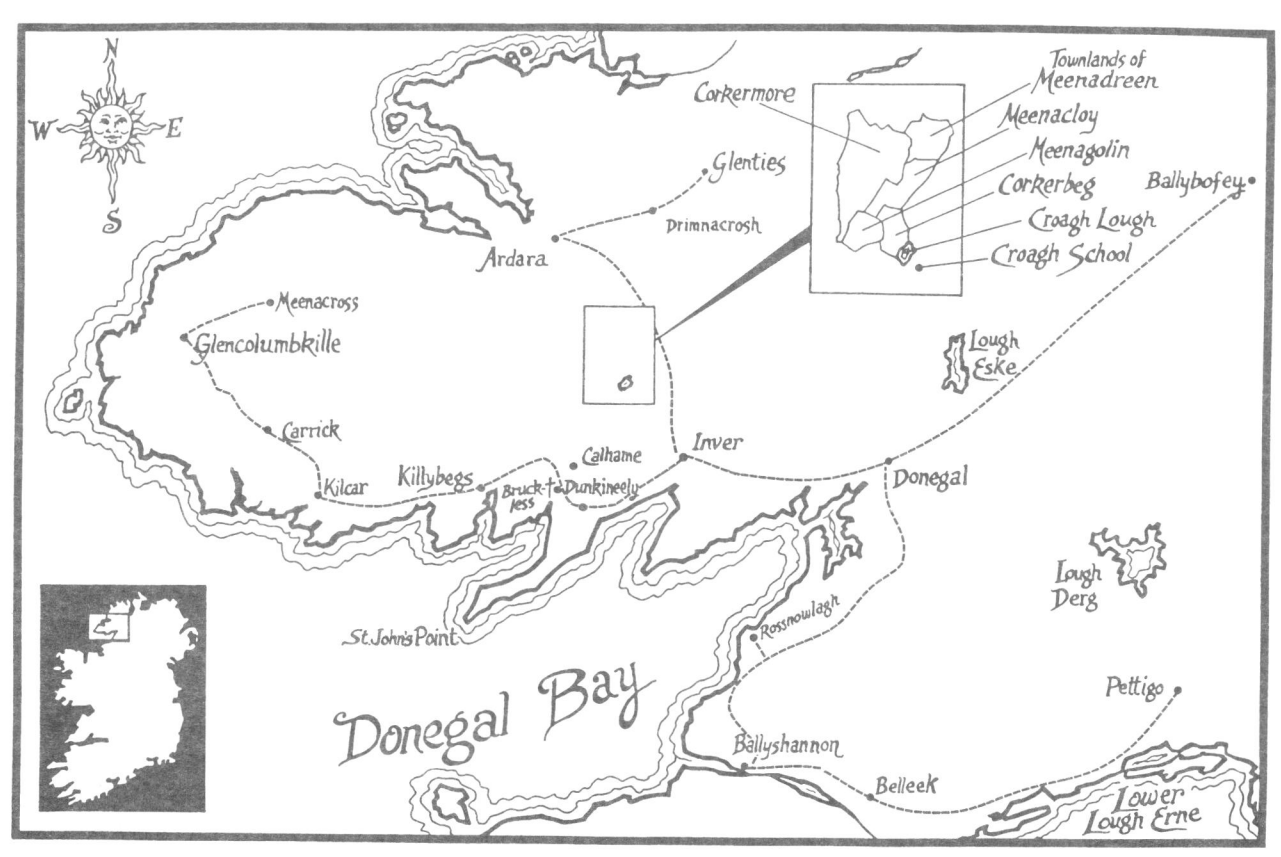

Southwest Donegal, Packie Manus' home territory. Map by Pierre Renaud reproduced by permission of Roger Millington Publishing.

1. Forgetting the lesson

A simple jig of great beauty

'My mother might lilt that when she was spinning, or when she was making tea, or something. She never stopped. The only time she wasn't lilting or humming or singing was when asleep, eating and in church. But for the rest of her life she lilted and sang.

When we were getting boisterous, she would start to lilt and get us dancing. Oh, she had several ways of ruling us: one of course was the knuckles. Another was, she would start to sing, especially when she was spinning. That was a good time, we could shout and do whatever we liked when she was spinning, because she couldn't get away from the thread and the pedals, but as soon as we would get anywhere near the wheel, we would get one right in the ear, and by heck she had hard knuckles. It was like getting hit with a smith's hammer!

She didn't have any name for it. I called it *Forgetting the lesson* because I was more interested in tunes than I was in education, and I suppose old McDyer[16] gave me a wallop for not paying attention. I was probably whistling a tune when he was talking, and that wouldn't do.'

It is fitting that the name of this jig concerns lapses of memory, because it seems that Packie himself forgot it for many years! In all the home recording sessions over the past decade and a half, during which Packie would rack his brains for tunes for us, this one never made an appearance. The way that we came by it is evidence of its catchiness. At the tail end of our visit to Packie in 1994, during an afternoon session in Peter Oliver's bar in Ardara, Packie played it quietly to himself on the whistle at a moment when everyone's attention was engaged in a group discussion. The tune imprinted itself in Steve's subconscious mind, and back in Canada he sang it over the transatlantic telephone to Packie, who told him it was a tune lilted by his mother. The following year, it turned up on the compilation cassette released by Veteran, FROM DONEGAL AND BACK! The version from that recording is given here.

---

16. James McDyer, the schoolmaster at Croagh school, which Packie attended until the age of fourteen.

2. McShane's rambles

Adapted by Packie from the air of the song by the same name

This fine jig, one of Packie's perennial favourites, has passed into limited circulation among Irish musicians, largely through Sharon Creasey, who learned the tune from Packie in the mid 1980s, and who passed it, along with **Stepping stones**, no. 5, to a number of musicians, including fiddler Lucy Farr, who recorded it on her 1992 cassette **HEART AND HOME** (Veteran VT123).

Packie has always maintained that he got the tune from Mr Collins, a traveller, during an impromptu roadside music and singing session in the late 1940s[17]. When we questioned Packie more closely about the tune's origins, however, he admitted that his version of the tune is a substantial reworking of what "old man Collins" played on the melodeon that afternoon more than fifty years ago.

> 'There's a story to this tune, and in fact there's a whole big long song to it. It was a kind of drunken song, you know. Let me think, now...'

---

17. The story of this encounter is told in **RECOLLECTIONS OF A DONEGAL MAN**, p. 124.

My name is McShane from the plains of Kildare
A farmer I was as until the last year
When I took a notion of higher promotion
Went over to England the harvest to share
Rum toora-la, rum toora-laddy
And rum toora-lam and shurrum toora-lay

I landed in Liverpool early one morning
Just as the natives were starting their day
There was some of them laughing, some of them chaffing
And the rest of them trying to chase Paddy away
Oh rum toora la, etc.

I met with a woman, I asked her for lodging
She says, my bould Pucko, my house it is full
But if you care to go to a woman I know
Who lives at a pub called The Big Spotted Bull

I went to this woman, I told her my story,
She quickly showed me a bed in a room
And I being dreary, footsore and weary,
I laid meself down for to banish me gloom

But a massive big tinker stood up in the corner
Swore by his soul he would kill all was there
Says I, my young lagging, give over your bragging
For I'm big McShane from the plains of Kildare

He tried for to hit me a belt in the stomach
I quickly landed him one in the throat
He fell in a heap and went soundly to sleep
After cracking his skull on a big chamberpot

He lay there not heeding, like a pig he was bleeding
I thought for my soul I had taken his life
So I ran to the bar, I came back with a jar
And meself and the tinker soon ended our strife

'You know it's about forty years since I sung that! The tune is slightly different to the air of this song. How did it come to be a jig? I think that old man Collins used to play the air of the song as a jig. I reworked the jig to put it out of people's knowing and still call it *McShane's rambles!*'

3. The storm

A popular tune with Donegal musicians in Packie's youth

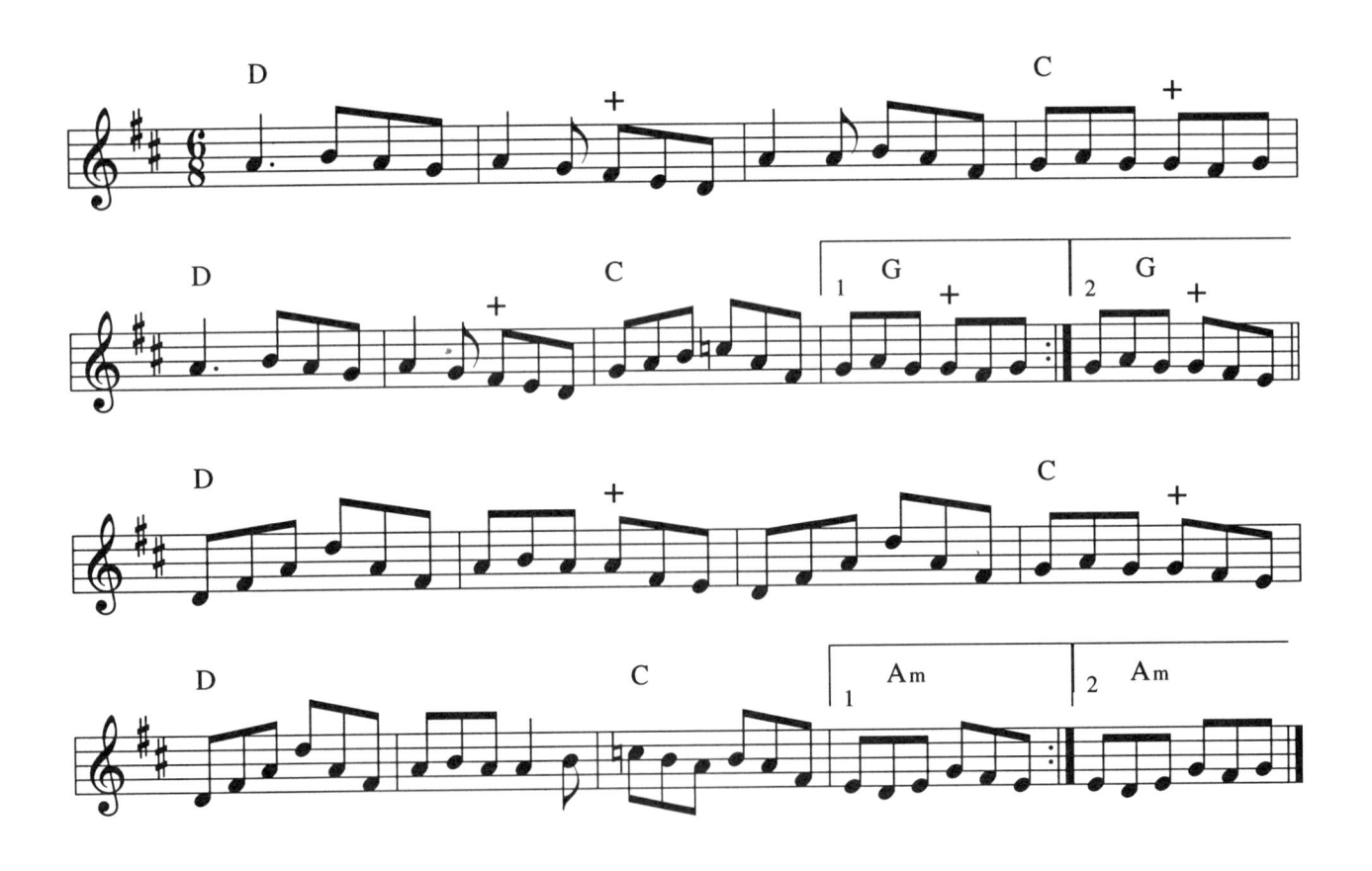

This simple and charming tune bears a distinct family resemblance to the well-known "big" tune from the Donegal fiddling tradition, *The king of the pipers*.

'That was a uillean piper's tune, an old tune that was going the rounds long before I was born. I just picked it up listening to people playing it. Big Pat used to play it—the name came from Big Pat—and the Dohertys, although I never heard John Doherty play it; but Mickey used to play it. I forgot about the tune, and when I started doing clubs with Felix Doran in England, he used to play it. I didn't teach it to Felix, oh no, it was just in his repertoire.

This tune may have other names in other areas. That's the trouble with traditional tunes. I often sat in a session where someone would mention a tune that I thought I didn't know, but when they'd start playing it I'd discover it was one that I knew by a different name. It gives you a good feeling to be able to join in!'

Keele folk festival in England in 1965. Packie Manus (at right) performing with the famous travelling piper Felix Doran (centre), with whom Packie played for a number of years, and another giant of Irish music, Sligo fiddler Michael Gorman. Photo: Brian Shuel.

4. The dark girl dressed in blue

The air to an American song

'That was from an old American song. My aunt Mary Byrne had the song with her back from America—she worked for a company in South Carolina. We never learned it because we thought it was silly, and I turned it into a jig, because the jig was more palatable than the song. Och, I was only a kid at the time. I think the song was in waltz time, and I don't remember the words...

> She was a fine girl, fol de diddle i do
> She was a fine girl, I tell you
> She was a fine girl, fol de diddle i do
> She was the dark girl dressed in blue

A lot of American songs would be turned into jigs and reels or hornpipes by some smart-arsed Irishman or woman!'[18]

Photo: Stephen Jones.

---

18. In this case, the "smart-arsed Irishman" in question is Packie himself.

5. Stepping stones

Adapted by Packie from a fragment played by shepherds

* Third only if wanted

'I think this was originally a mountain whistler's tune: in the old days, getting the dogs to round up sheep, they never spoke to the dogs, you know. They done it all by whistling.

And there was dogs [that] would work to certain tunes—now this is true! And there are horses that would take notice of certain tunes, and there are cows: if you're milking a cow, and you're singing a certain tune, she'll be quite quiet, and when you stop she'll send you, the pail of milk and all flying! We've had animals like that at home. They got so used to me mother singing for them when she would be milking them, if a stranger would try, they would put you out of the shed.

I can't remember where I picked this up. I think the jig is my version of the tune. The whistling one was not in proper jig time... [whistles the tune in free time] ...and a certain dog would know that whistle, and if you or I tried it, that dog wouldn't take a blind bit of notice, but if his master whistled it, the dog would start a round of work. It amuses me when I watch sheepdog trials here on telly, and somebody will whistle an order. I don't know a damn how dogs can understand that, but they do. And then people'll laugh at the idea of them understanding jigs and reels and things, but they do!

Stepping stones was a name I just thought of. At our place, before the bridge was built we had to cross the river on stepping stones — *clocháins* in Gaelic.'

The version of this tune that has passed into limited circulation among Irish musicians is in E. However, the earliest version played by Packie, and the one he prefers, is in D. The first part of a jig recorded by James Kelly and Paddy O'Brien as *The horse's leotard* bears an uncanny resemblance to this tune.

6. The Byrnes of Gleann Cholm Cille

A "family" tune passed down through the ages

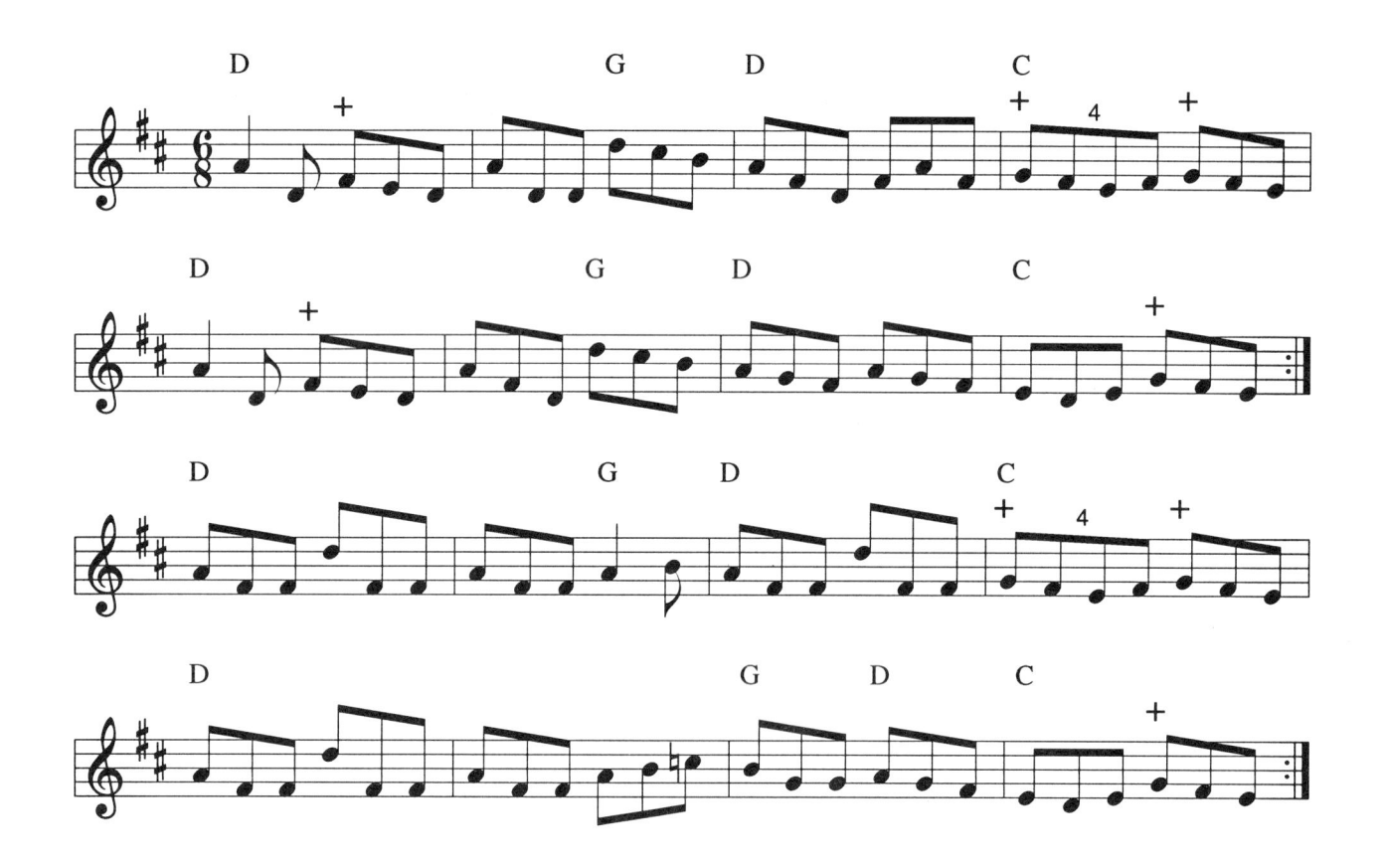

'All my Byrne relations were involved in blacksmithing, and many of them were from Gleann Cholm Cille, way out at the west point of Donegal. Each branch of the family all had their own set of tunes that came down through the generations, and this one arrived with Big Pat. He played it in his younger days. Maybe I don't remember it exactly as he played it, I may have changed it about a bit.'

7. Merry hours of gladness

A well-known song tune transformed into a jig

'That is a jig version of the air to the song *Oh the days of the Kerry dancing*, a very well known south of Ireland song. It was recorded by John McCormack in his early days. That was put into a jig by someone, I don't know who—not by me.'

8. Crossing the Oily river

Packie's setting of a tune enjoying renewed popularity

'This is one of those tunes that died out and then got a revival: it's played by James Byrne, and it's played by the Ó Maonaigh family, and the Glackins.'

The first part of this version is virtually identical to that recorded by Altan on THE RED CROW as *Con Cassidy's*, but Packie's turn or second part is quite different. Packie had no name for it, but coined this title during our visit in February 1997.

'The Oily river flows down near Big Pat's house. It was crossed on stepping stones. Now the Corker river is on the other side of the hill from Meenbug.[19] At one place there is about half a mile or so of difference between them. Then they were all called the Corker river one time, till they went down as far as a place called Currafeehan or down to Drumdubh, which means the black back, and then became the Oily river, but actually the start of the Oily river passes by Big Pat's house. Nearly all the rivers in our area had English names. The big river in Inver was called the Eany, and that is not a Gaelic word.'[20]

---

19. Meenbug ("the soft plain") was the name given to the small central area of the townland of Corkermore where Packie's parents and neighbours lived.

20. "Eany" is in fact derived from the Irish *eanach*, meaning a watery place, pond or lake, marsh or swamp.

9. A dossan of heather

A tune from Big Pat

'That was one of Big Pat's, at least he used to play it, and I think it was him that called it the *Dossan of heather.*

A *dossan*[21] is a stalk of heather, a big sprig of heather, or a tuft. That's a word that's used in Scotland. We'd use dossans of heather for making brooms, besoms. You went to the hill and pulled the dossan up out of the ground. We used to use them for whitewashing, for putting the lime on the outside of the house. And also for spraying potatoes. You had your bucket of spray and you dipped the besom into it and shook it over the potatoes. It was slow work, but it worked.

Funny then, that moved from the heather to people. Young lads, if their parents weren't forever after them telling them right from wrong they would never bother getting their hair cut—and very often it would be the parents themselves would cut the hair. My mother would say, "Sit down here till I take off your dossan." If they saw somebody with a big head of hair: "He had a great dossan."'

Several versions of this tune appear on our tapes, most having two parts, but some having three. During our visit to Packie in 1997, however, he insisted that there should be four parts: "Probably I didn't play it properly. There may be some other way of playing the fourth part different from the second." This being so, with Packie's blessing Jean modified the second part to create a distinct fourth part.

---

21. The word comes from the Irish *dos*, meaning a tuft. The derivative form *dossán* is used frequently in Irish and also by English speakers.

10. Teelin rowdies

A Packie Manus composition

'Oh, that's one of mine all right. I can swear to that'un! It wouldn't be one of the first ones I made up, because when I got to know what rowdies were, and probably got involved with them at times, I would be full grown. Maybe shortly before I went away to England, when I was almost twenty.

Teelin is a fishing area, and all fishing areas at one time had their quota of rowdies. A rowdy is a man that nobody wants to tangle with. There was the Gleann Cholm Cille rowdies, there was the Teelin rowdies, and St. John's Point, there were rowdies there, and Inver rowdies, and the whole county—right away down the Rosses, Burtonport and Bunbeg—they all had their share of rowdies, and round here too. The fishermen were tough characters. They had to be to survive in a little open boat with an oar. If a big storm came on you had to be a rowdy to take the boat home.

Now there's a funny thing, they would pick a fight with anybody but not with each other. I never yet heard of say the Teelin lot and the St. John's Point lot having any squabble at all, and they were meeting out at big days and religious demonstrations and all, but you never heard of them fighting, but they would knock hell out of any other one they met! They weren't blood relations, but they were occupational relations: they would fish in the same area.

It was funny about the fishermen: they were all very generous people. You would take them now to be a tough hard lot that didn't give a damn about anybody, but they would go out of their way to do you a good turn. And do you know it still applies, there's something about the fisher people. I think it is because always when they come in, they're thanking God that they didn't hit a storm, and they're all back safe. And if they can do something for somebody they'll do it. Drunk or sober. And most of the time drunk, when they're in... [laughs].'

Photo: Stephen Jones.

11. The sheigh o' rye

Another Packie Manus composition. Simple but lovely.

'Rye is a crop we used to grow around here, and when it was nicely milled it made beautiful bread, good strong bread. Who gave it that name? I did. Why? Because I made it up, and probably it reminded me of a sheigh[22] of rye, if somebody was building a rye stack. They'd place the sheaves side by side: that way one or a few sheaves could be removed without tumbling the stack.'

---

22. Sheaf.

12. The sapper

A tune from Big Pat based on the song "D'ye ken John Peel"

'Big Pat used to play that for part of a set dance that he called "the sapper." He probably thought it up himself out of the John Peel tune: he called it *John Peel's Farewell*. The sapper was one part of a set—they call it "a basket" in England. Four people would swing around. They kept the beat going with their feet, and the tune had to be in jig time. The three repeated notes at the start of the second part was the bang! bang! bang! and they were away then into the tapping time.

Now, the sapper: they were people that used to go round cutting out brands on stones along the road, milestones, and also the boundary of your land. They didn't build fences away back in the old days. Cattle and sheep ran amok. But then they started dividing the lands, and the sappers used to come around and dot out your boundary.'

13. The lazy wife

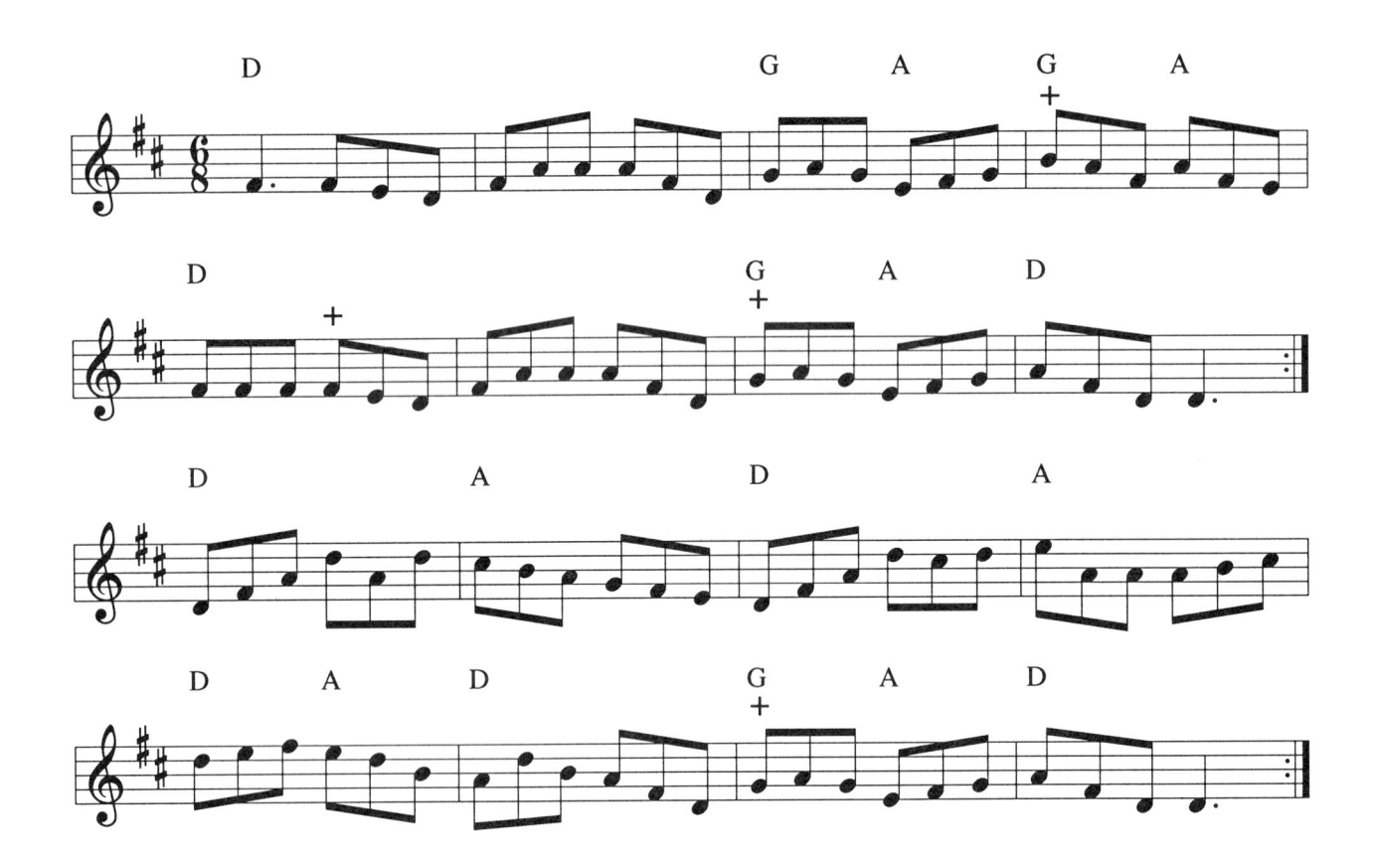

'This tune reminds me of some of my father's stories—one in particular:

A hard-working man had a very lazy wife who stayed in bed nearly all the time. He tried every way he could think of but still she refused to do any housework. Now, this happened long before pyjamas or night-dresses were the fashion, when women wore what they called "shifts" in bed. A shift was a long garment (most were of home-made material) tied with ribbons down the front.

One morning he decided to shame her into doing some work, so he got up early and put his plan into action, went to the bed and said: "I have a pot of water boiling, the clothes are in the tub outside the door, the soap is on the windowsill and it's a great day for washing." She hopped out of bed, took off her shift, threw it at him and said, "Give that a dip while you're at it," and went back to bed.'

14. Willie dear

One of Packie's favourite jigs

'As far as I remember, I took that from the air of an old traditional song that Big Biddy Sweeney, my mother's aunt, used to sing. I never learned the words, and I'm sorry now because 'twas a lovely thing. It had something to do with a girl that dressed up as a man and joined a ship. So, sooner than let it die out altogether I turned it into a jig.

> Oh hold your tongue dear Captain
> Your talk it is all in vain
> For once I had a true love
> And for him I have crossed the main
>
> And if I do not find him, well
> I'll mourn him constantly
> And for the sake of Willie dear
> A maid I'll always be

That was Big Bridget's song, and I think that was the name of it, *Willie dear*. These songs were in a kind of a cluster amongst ourselves.'

There were two Biddy Sweeneys, both fine singers, living in the area where Packie was brought up. The source of this song was "Big" Bridget, née Gallagher, and Packie's great aunt. The other was no relation, and has a tune in this collection named after her (**Barefoot Biddy**, no. 69).

15. Showers of autumn

'I was at a party in a hotel in Donegal a couple of months ago for a cousin of mine, she's ninety years. She's a Mrs Boyle. She was asking me if I remembered any of the old songs that were going around when we were young. She had ten brothers and they were all singers. She danced that night with her grandsons!

Now her brother was a great fiddler player, and that was one of his favourite tunes. He was Manus Gallagher and he went away to America in his young days, but before he went away he was a nice fiddle player, and his brother Peter was a good fiddle player. Probably I learned the tune from Manus Gallagher.

It's a very mild sort of a tune! It might be a Scottish tune, because a lot of the old folk in our area went to Scotland for the winter months, and they had no entertainment, except they brought their fiddles over with them, and they swapped tunes with the Scottish people. That might be one that came back from Scotland. I wouldn't think that Manus Gallagher went to Scotland, but his father did, and my father did.'

16. Foyne's legacy

This tune and the following one were recorded on the 1969 EFDSS LP **Packie Byrne**.

'Foyne was a landlord at one time. I think he was an Englishman. He wasn't in this area. I won't say this for sure, but I think he was from Sligo, Mayo or Galway, somewhere on that west coast. He wasn't too kind to his tenants, as a lot of the landlords weren't in those days. So the tenants threatened him, with the result that he got so scared that he divided up his land and his money among the people, and they christened the tune *Foyne's legacy*. I don't know how the tune came into the story—probably someone composed it when all this was going on.'

17. Away and over

'That's an old fishermen's tune. It was going around when I was born, I suppose. When the homemade sailboats first started, they didn't have a perpendicular pull with a swing arm or anything. They just had a pole up the front of the boat and a pole up the stern, and this pole across. And you used to draw the sheet up over this pole and tie it down on one side, and if the wind changed they had to loose that rope and run round and tie it on the other side. "Away and over" they used to shout when the rope would go over.'

This tune is closely related to the air of the Scottish song, *Give me a lass with a lump of land*.

18. I'll marry you when me garden grows

The air to a song, *My fair lady*, popular when Packie was young

I'll marry you when me garden grows
Don't care if everybody knows
Everything now is out in rows
A-pointing to the sun

There'll be lots to eat for you and me
And maybe for a family
So I'll marry you when me garden grows
My fair lady

'That's a song that was sung around here when I was young. I never bothered learning it, because as soon as I heard the words "my fair lady", I thought, I'm not wasting my time with that! I think Delia Murphy used to sing it, and some of the famous tenors used to sing it in the old days.

My father used to tell a story about two men that fancied the same girl. They both spent a lot of time planting, weeding and making their gardens as nice as possible, because in those days a nice garden was a sign of happiness, contentment and wealth, and often girls fell in love with the man who owned the garden without ever meeting him. However, one of the men decided to destroy the other's garden, so he spent a whole night carrying buckets of water from the sea and splashing it over the other man's flowers and plants, killing the lot. He wasted his time, because the girl married a hedge-cutter.'

19. The peeler and the goat

A policeman meets his match

The satirical song of which this is the tune was composed by Diarmaid Ó Riain (Darby Ryan, 1770-1855), born near the village of Bansha in Tipperary. The local police officer (the "Bansha peeler") is held up to ridicule through the story of his encounter with a goat whom he tries to arrest. The song is well enough known, but the tune makes a fine jig and deserves to be more widely heard.

20. Socks on the crane

Recreated from an incomplete tune on tape

This tune appears on one of our home recordings in incomplete form. On hearing the fragments in 1997, Packie was unable to recall the tune, but approved of our suggestion that Jean should salvage it by writing in the missing bars.

> 'I'll tell you what, you keep that part that you fleshed out, join them together, and we'll have a decent jig.'

Packie named the tune in response to the comment that the first part was reminiscent of the old three-part piping jig, *The pipe on the hob*. The crane was an iron frame used for hanging cooking pots over the fire, but doubled as a clothes-drying rack.

> 'The crane was a great invention, because when you had a big heavy pot full of spuds—maybe a half hundredweight of spuds in one great big pot—this crane was worked so that you could draw it out, it opened like a gate. The big pot was boiling mad and it was going to put the water out and do away with the fire, and you just pulled out the crane, and there was no lifting the big heavy pot. The Irish were not educated, but by heck they could think things out, you know! It was the art of survival.'

Photo: Reinhard Goerner.

21. The wheels of the train

The air of a song with a misleading title

'Anyone would think that the "wheels of the train" meant the rollers on a railway train, but it doesn't.

In the old days, the brides on their wedding day wore very long dresses, coming along on the ground, maybe two or three yards behind them. There was nearly always one or two little youngsters that carried this. They called it the train. There were little balls of cotton, about two or three inches in diameter, sewn into the cloth, so that these little balls came hopping along on the ground, and kept the train from becoming soaked with water and muck, dirt and so on. That's in case the young kids that carried the train made some mistake.

But there was one young lad that was not minding his business. He stepped on these little wheels, these puffs. I don't remember the complete story, whether it was that her dress fell off completely or tore into pieces, but he reckoned that he would never be seen at a wedding again. That was his first and last wedding. The song was called *The wheels of the train*.'

> My feet got caught in the wheels of her train
> And I'll never be seen at a wedding again

The song may have been very widely circulated: Jean's neighbour in rural Quebec, T.C. McNaughtan, told him that his father learned it from an old record and used to sing it during the 1920s or 1930s. The air appears to be derived from a jig published in KERR'S COLLECTION of MERRY MELODIES, Vol. 2, as *The laird o' cockpen* (no. 306).

Photo: Stephen Jones.

22. The half door

A classic Packie tune

Packie plays this air and jig on the 1977 Dingle's Records album of the same name, made with Bonnie Shaljean. The air is the air to a song, the story of which is told below. The jig is widely known, although its name is not.[23] As is often the case, Packie's second part is quite different from the one commonly played.

> 'This chap was making his way home from a fair, and he struck up an acquaintance with a young girl. As they were passing her house it started raining, so she invited him to come into the house. He went in, and had tea, and currant cake, and he saw her father's fiddle hung over the fireplace, so he took it down and started playing a tune. She ran and left the tea and took off the half door, which was really meant for dancing on, and laid it on the earthen floor, and put on her shoes, and started dancing. That went on for a while, and when he was leaving she came down the boreen a bit with him towards the road and he asked her to marry him, and they were married and lived happily ever after. That's a shortened version of the story, but *The half door* is a really nice tune.
>
> I learned this long ago, and like a lot of songs and tunes, I forgot about it I suppose until I met a family called the Grehan sisters. I was living in Manchester at the time and they came to live in the same house, three sisters. They were good performers and good musicians, from Boyle in County Roscommon, and they used to sing *The half door* in the clubs.'

---

23. The tune has been recorded by Tommy Peoples as *Pat Burke's jig*.

23. An t-éan sa chrann

Big Pat's variant of a widely known tune

'*An t-éan sa chrann* means "the bird in the tree". There's another tune called *The bird in the bush*, but when you hear the other tune you always hear the title in English.

I can't remember where I learned that, but I'm sure Big Pat played that tune. There were a lot of birds around our place, different kinds in the winter and in the summer.'

A cousin of two better-known jigs, *The tenpenny bit,* and one known under several titles, recorded by the Chieftains as *Ballinasloe fair* and also widely known as *The lilting banshee*. The other tune to which Packie refers is the well-known reel recorded by Michael Coleman as *The bird in the tree*.

24. An fear dall

A Packie Manus composition

'I composed this tune, when I was at school maybe. *An fear dall* means "the blind man", because when I was playing it, it sounded like a blind man searching his way. I gave it a Gaelic name, because that was commonly done. In the old days, nearly all the old jigs and reels in this area got Gaelic names, but later on they got Englified!'

25. The buckasheen landy

A well-known tune, but with an entertaining local title

'A buckasheen[24] is the name given to a young lad when he would take the first notion of women, when he decided that it was time he was experimenting with the opposite sex. He would be out at night grabbing women, and he hadn't a great technique because he had no practice, and he would think that maybe by strength he could badger down the women to his way of thinking. They called him "buckasheen landy" because "landy" is a polite word for "randy"!

---

24. The word comes from the Irish *boc*, literally a goat, but also used to mean a lively young fellow or "buck". "Buckasheen" is an anglicized diminutive corresponding to the use of the Irish suffix *-ín*.

Did I associate the tune with any particular buckasheen that I knew? I didn't, because we were all buckasheens, and landy!

My father used to lilt that tune [demonstrates], and then he would run out of breath, he was very bad with asthma, and he would stop, take a great long breath and start it up again. This went on for some time, and when he would stop again, you would think, Thank God it's over. But no, the pause, the gasp, and he was off again!'

This tune appears in a three-part setting as *Daniel of the sun* in O'Neill's THE DANCE MUSIC OF IRELAND, no. 200.

26. The collier laddie

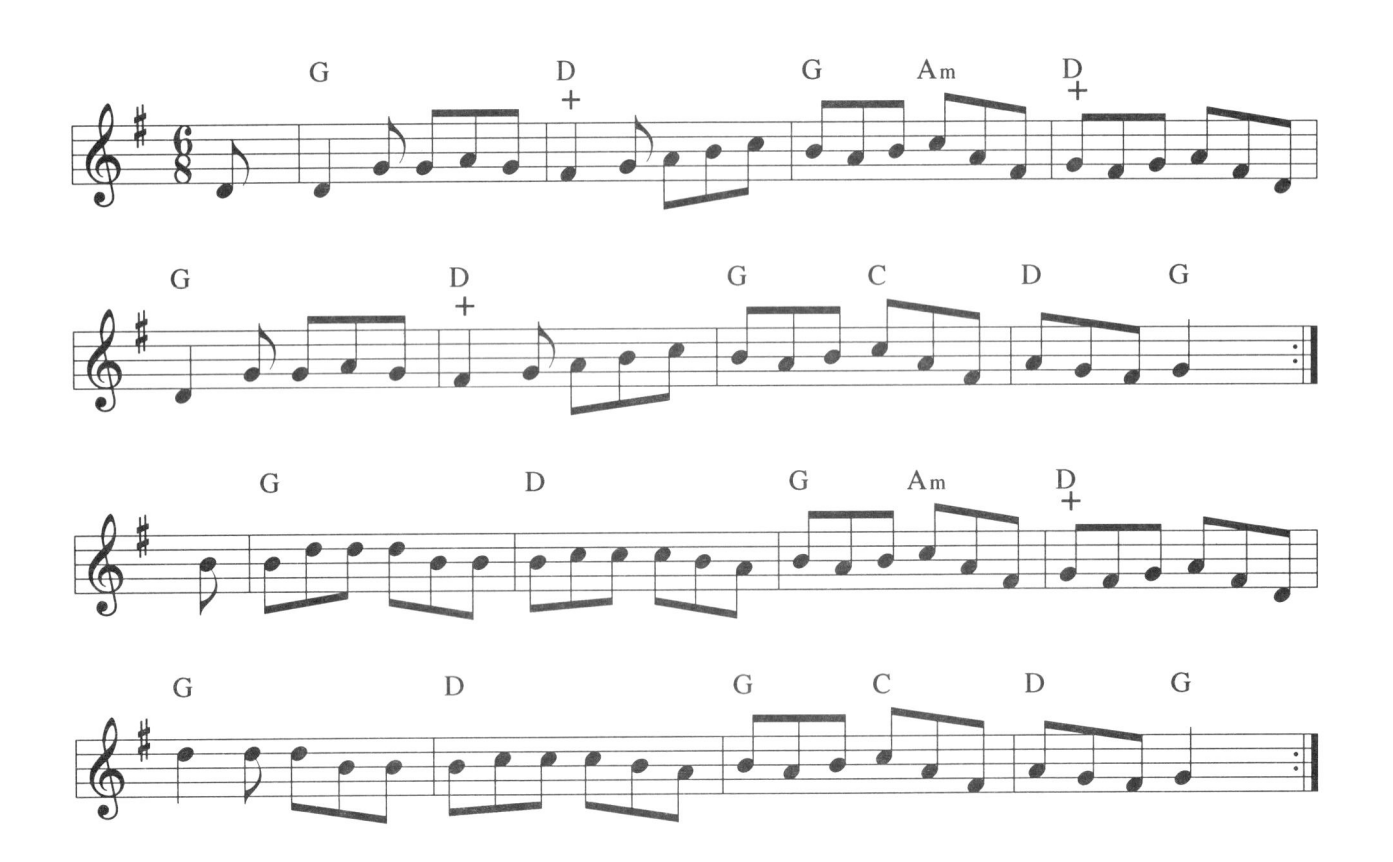

'That's a Scottish tune. It probably came over with the tatty hokers.[25] There is a song by the same name that is very popular in the north of England, but this tune has nothing to do with the air of that song. But it is similar to another song called *The recruited collier* [sung by Bonnie Shaljean on **The Half Door**], and who knows, maybe some clever bugger put the song Bonnie sings to that air.'[26]

---

25. Potato lifters. See the text accompanying **The tatty hokers**, no. 68.

26. "Some clever bugger": doubtless the same person as the "smart-arsed Irishman or woman" referred to in no. 4!

27. Paddy Bhilli *na rópaí*

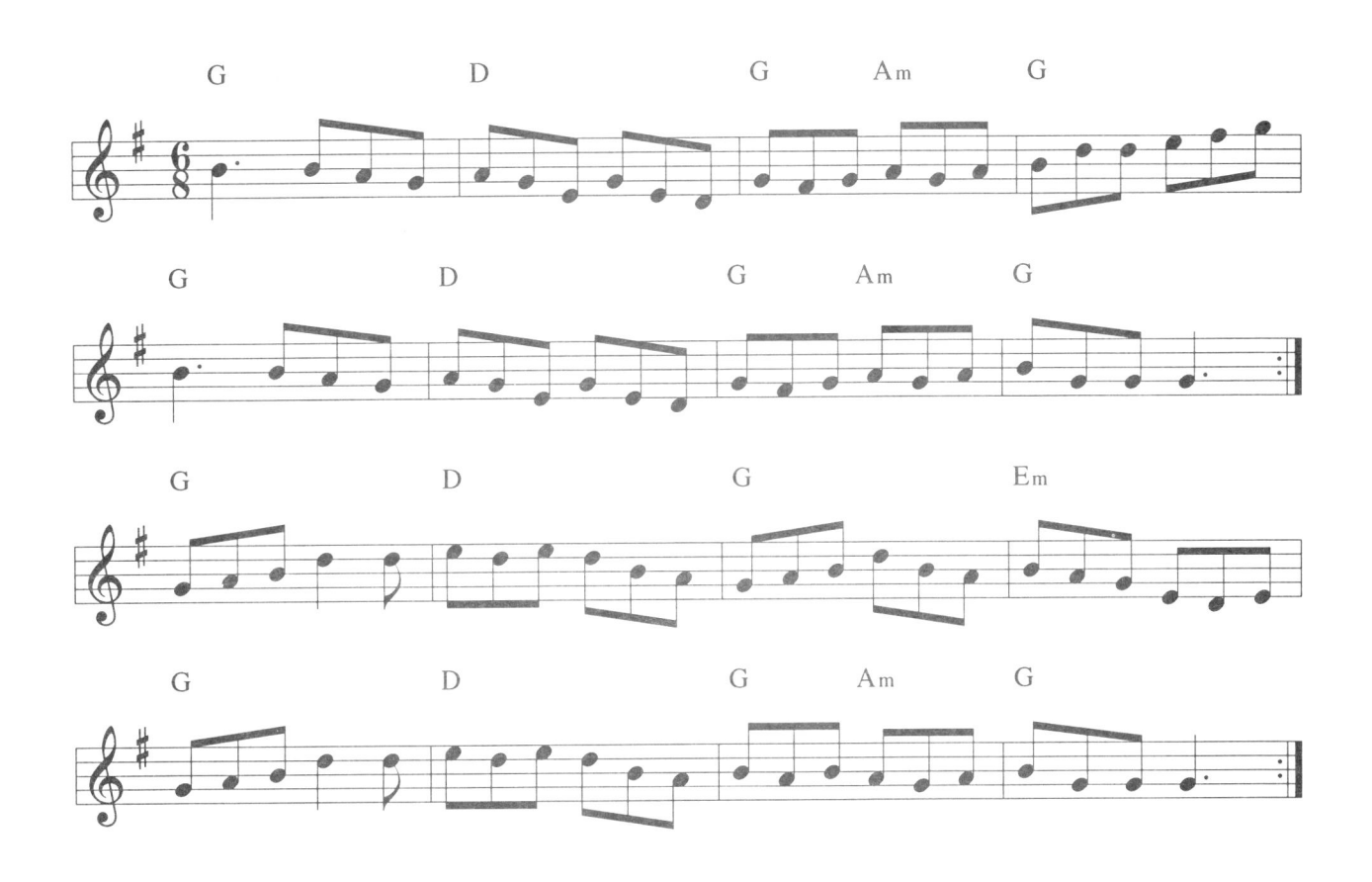

This tune is named after Paddy Boyle, a prominent fiddle player in southwest Donegal during the early part of the twentieth century.[27]

> 'The reason this tune has Paddy Boyle's name is that he used to play it very often. He went round to schools and local dance halls playing his fiddle. In our area there were four or five different turns of the set, and each turn had its own tune. When it came to jig time, that was the tune he would play for the dancers, so it was known as Paddy Boyle's jig.
>
> Paddy was born out around Kilcar or Carrick and came to live in Calhame at an early age. Paddy *na rópaí* means "Paddy of the ropes", because his father used to make ropes. The ropes were made out of fir sticks—they would dig the fir up out of the bog and beat it down, and then they would hand-plait the fibres into ropes. One of them ropes would last maybe twenty years. They would be mostly used for keeping roofs down.'

---

27. See **Recollections of a Donegal Man**, pp. 82–83.

Slip jigs

'I was as big as I am today when I first saw a slip jig danced. They weren't very popular at all, and I think the reason was that the slip jig wasn't noisy enough. You couldn't really do enough footwork, besides the ordinary jig: that was great, you could knock hell out a big flag floor, but the slip jig was kind of tame. It's still tame! And you wouldn't get many musicians to play slip jigs.'

Despite these somewhat disparaging remarks about slip jigs, Packie is fond of this type of tune, and three out of the four examples presented here are his compositions.

28. *An cailín rua* (The red-haired girl)

Composed by Packie and named after his cousin Kitty

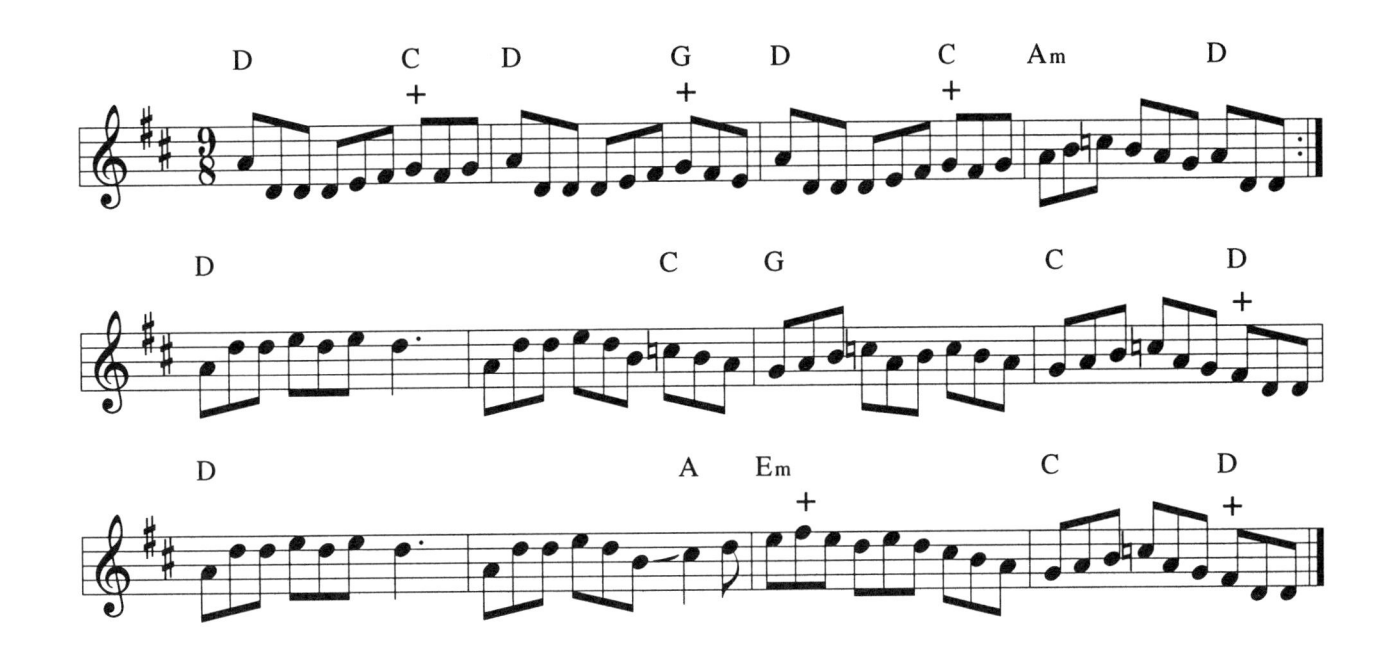

'Kitty Byrne was the sister of a fellow that we were talking about to that woman and man at the table today—Charlie Byrne. His sister was blood-red haired. It was an unusual red, because it was nearly a mahogany red, and 'twas right down past her waist; when she sat down she would lift it in case she sat on it, and it was one ringlet after another. I remember when she was a wee kid, and the mother would be trying to comb her hair and you'd hear her crying out at the road, the ringlets were so tight that the mother couldn't get the comb through her hair, and she was screaming in pain. Kitty was a lovely-looking girl, so I dedicated the tune to her. She went away to America when she was a teenager. She's dead now.'

29. Piddling Peggy

An attractive and curiously named slip jig composed by Packie Manus

This Packie Manus composition has a real Donegal flavour to it. Packie also plays it as a highland (see no. 42).

'People laugh to this day when I tell them the name of that tune, and they think it means that Peggy was piddling, but she wasn't! Piddlin' was a kind of a corrupt name for a game called "peidealing". Now a *peideal*[28] is a Gaelic name for a little pebble, or a *cloch bheag*. To play this game of pebbling, you put a little pebble on the nail of your thumb and you flicked it like that. If you could hit a little pole stuck in the ground, you were the outright winner. All the pebbles made a circle round the pole, and there was a bloke there with a little measure, and he measured the distance from the pole to the pebbles. The one that was nearest the post won.

---

28. *Peideal* is not to be found in dictionaries of Irish, ancient or modern. The word has been attested to by an Irish speaker from the Gleann Cholm Cille area, but in the view of Liam Ó Cuinneagáin, this is a typical case of an English word (in this case, "pebble") mispronounced by native Irish speakers, many of whom had little English. See the Note on Irish orthography, p. 22.

This Peggy McGee, she became a champion at flicking these pebbles. She was from a bit nearer Ardara than our place. I think she was from around Carrickacleaba or somewhere away up there on the Donegal road. The Gaelic word became a bit mixed up, and it finished up as "peddle" instead of *peideal*, like a cross between pebble and *peideal*. She was called "Peidealing Peggy", but she was also known as "Piddling Peggy". She won all the championships in our area for years and years. She was the champion piddler around us!'

Readers may form their own opinion as to the veracity of this story. Packie, however, insists that not only did Peggy McGee exist, but that she was indeed a formidable exponent of the pebble-flicking game. On other tellings, Packie has asserted that the object of the game was to get pebbles into a jam jar. This adds a comic element to the story, when told to introduce a performance of the tune, in which Peggy is described as "peidealing" into a jam jar.

Photo: Stephen Jones.

30. The dawn pack

Composed by Packie Manus

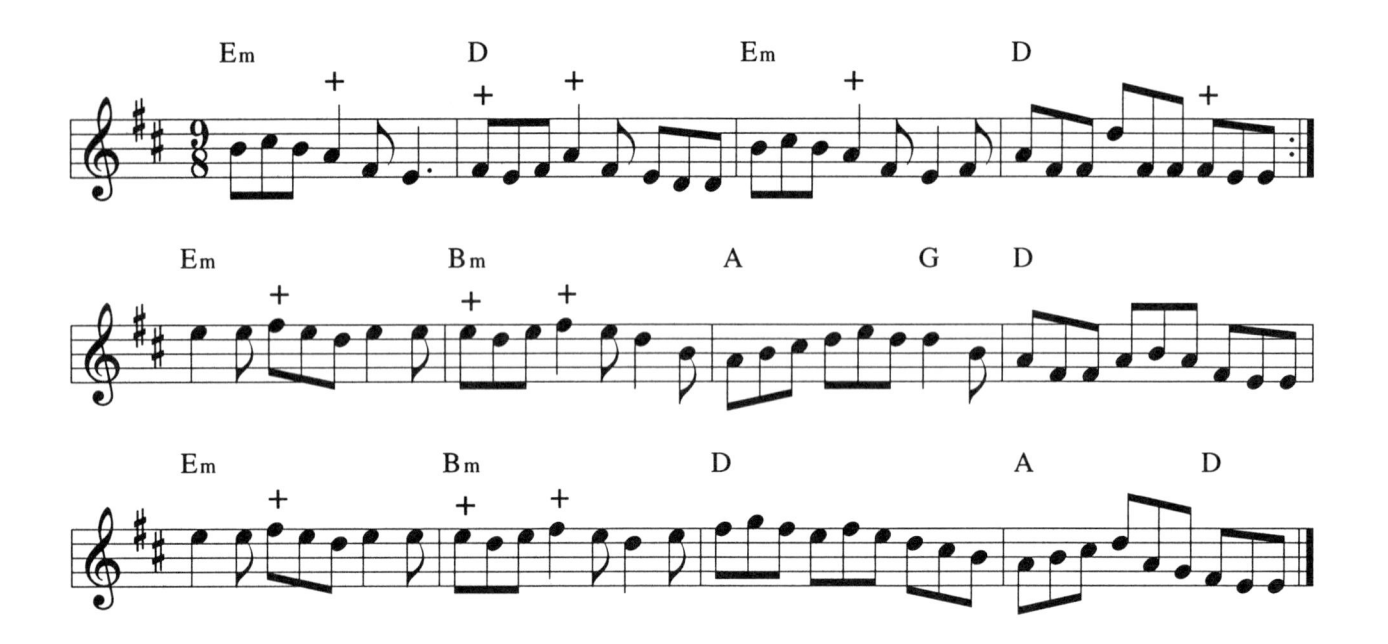

'Away back in history, in the old days when they used to hunt wild boars, and stags, and elks, they had two packs of hounds because one pack wouldn't be fit to stand the abuse of the whole day. They had one pack came out at dawn and one at noon. The dawn pack had to work from dawn to noon, and the other from noon to dark.

This was the aristocracy: they had horses and dogs. We didn't have horses or dogs in those days! They used to rack down fences and tumble stone walls, and they had men out cutting gaps in the stone walls, so that they could follow this elk. The farmers then had to be out building up the stone walls, and couldn't say a word. If they did they were dead.'

31. Humours of whiskey

Packie's version of a slip jig well known in Donegal

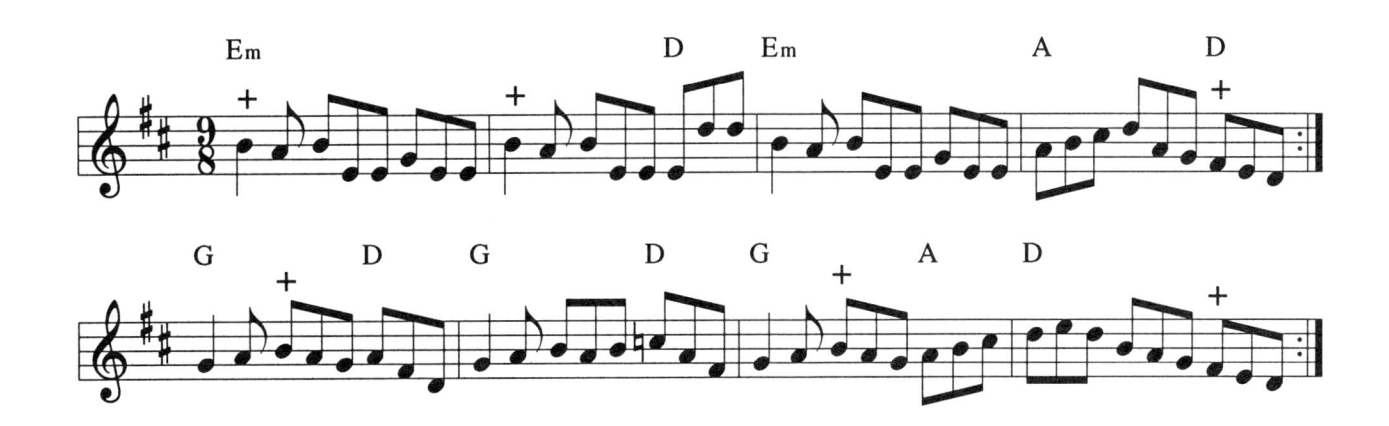

'Pat Kennedy used to play that on the melodeon. He was an old fellow that lived away down near Dunkineely. He was Patrick Kennedy, but we used to call him Uncle Pat, because he had a whole lot of nephews and nieces. I remember getting this tune from him when I was quite young; in later years I used to be down about his house, and he still used to play it as good as ever on one of the old three-stopper melodeons. That's the exact way he taught it to me. It was one of the very few slip jigs played in the area. He used to play it for a sapper dance, part of the set dance.[29]'

---

29. See **The sapper**, no. 12.

Marches and polkas

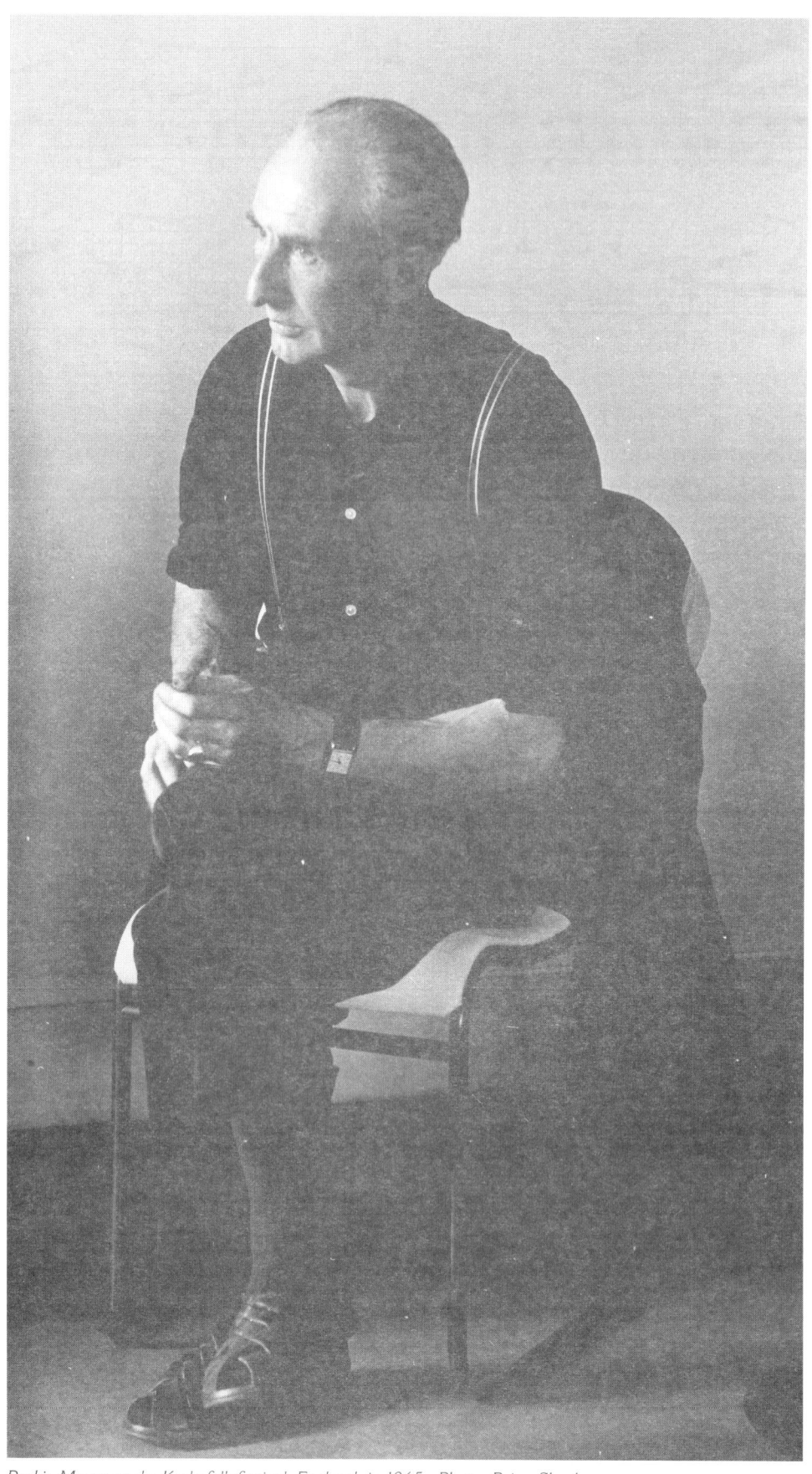

Packie Manus at the Keele folk festival, England, in 1965. Photo: Brian Shuel.

32. The Tummel march

'That's a Scottish march, a piping march, but do you know I never heard any Scots people play that march. It was just in our area—probably came over with migratory workers or tatty hokers. It's a nice tune, but there's not a whole lot to it. A lot of the Scottish marches don't have a great range, you know, because the highland pipes don't have a great range.

Alex Mackay, a man from Glasgow, told me the name of that tune, forty years ago when the folk scene first started, and I wrote it down on a piece of paper, and of course I lost it. Alex was down to his last farthing and I kept him for a week or two and gave him a bit of grub until he got digs. He called it *Tummel Takin*, or something like that. I was looking at a map, and I saw a lake called Tummel, and there's a town in Scotland called Tummel Bridge.'

33. The fumbling chorister (march)

A march made from a church hymn

To Jesus' heart all burning with fervent love for men
My heart with fondness yearning shall raise this joyful strain
While ages course along, this be with loudness sung
For the sacred heart of Jesus, by every heart and tongue

'I used to sing that when I was a youngster in the church choir. It's a nice air, but it breaks into a nice march. I remember there were girls in the choir with us. We were only small little fellas and they were all full-grown girls. We used to be groping them like hell, and they couldn't say a word, they had to carry on singing. Us with straight faces, oh dear!'

34. A besom of heather (polka)

A dossan of heather revisited

The jig **A dossan of heather** (no. 9) reappears here dressed as a polka. Since, as Packie explains, besoms were made from dossans, our name for the tune has a certain satisfying logic to it.

35. The belling march

A popular march in Donegal

Packie heard this tune played in Ardara by an accordion and fiddle band. He has no idea of where the name came from, except a vague notion that at one time the tune might have been played on hand bells.

36. I've got a bonnet (polka)

'That was a Scottish tune. It probably was something else when it was Scottish, I can't tell you anything about that tune, except that it's played for a polka in Ireland. It was being played when I was a toddler.'

37. Mín na hÉireann (march)

This family of tunes started life as a highland known as *Meenacurran*, or **Mín a'Churráin** (no. 45). When Packie made an air and march out of it, he changed the name to *Mín na hÉireann* (the plain of Ireland), because the name was easy to explain to his English folk-club audiences. The air and march are recorded on THE HALF DOOR. Only the march is transcribed here, since the air differs little except in tempo and ornamentation.

> 'The highland came first, because a fellow called Johnny Haughey used to play it on the fiddle in our area away back years ago. He was a farm labourer from out in the hills near Kilcar, a place called Gleann Baile Dubh, which means "the glen of the black road". Mín a'Churráin is a lake not so far from where I was born.'

38. Captain Taylor's march

A tune of local and historical interest

'Conyngham, he was the landlord in this area, because where I was born—Meenbug—was on the Marquis of Conyngham's estate. He was from Kent, and a very fine fellow he was too. I never remember him, but my father remembered him.

Another one then was Major Porter. Now he was a bad animal. There were several stories about Porter. Captain Taylor was a land steward for Porter, as far as I heard. Captain Taylor was very well liked, but he hadn't the full say, because Porter was the boss. And of course there was many a thing that Porter commanded his henchmen to do that young Captain Taylor wouldn't do, because he was too fond of the neighbours. He was a good musician: he used to play fiddle and he was a nice singer, and he became very popular. Only one or maybe two tunes of his ever survived, and this is one of them.'

Like **Mín na hÉireann** (no. 37), this tune is featured on THE HAlf DOOR as an air and march. We have not included the air version here, since it differs little from the march.

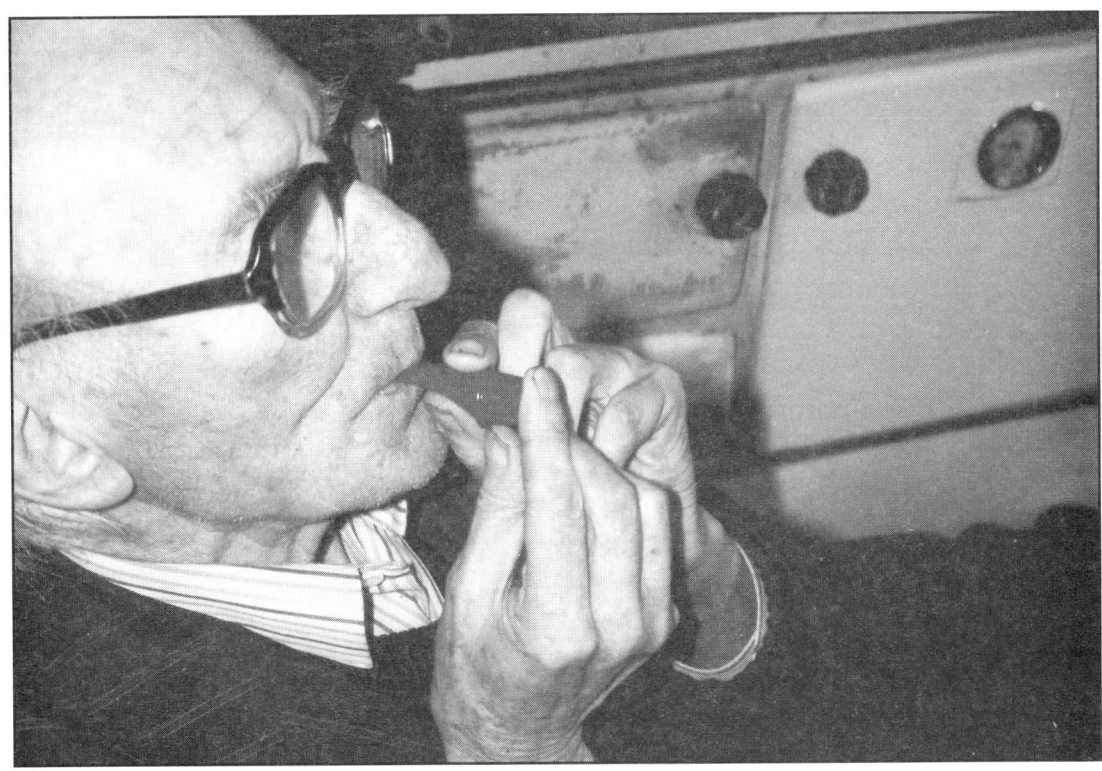

Packie Manus at 80 shows how to play a tune using only the mouthpiece of a whistle. Photo: Stephen Jones.

39. The swamp reed march

A "one-handed" whistle tune made by Packie for playing on a home-made reed whistle

'My brother Jim could make whistles out of boor tree—a white hazel tree—that's a very hard wood shell with a marrow, and you could poke out the marrow and burn holes, and make flutes. Jim also used to cut reeds on the back hills. We had reeds growing up in the swamps—swamp reeds. They were about as thick as a very small whistle. Boring the holes was nothing, but [to make the mouthpiece] he cut a kind of a slanting cut with my father's razor. My father then wondered what the hell happened to his razor, it wouldn't shave, but do you know my brother could make a right good job of them.

Now that tune, I used to play it with two whistles, one in each hand… play the melody on one and the harmony on the other. I also played it on a three-whistle outfit using the third whistle to play a continuous drone note—all very stupid-looking, but the club audiences loved it.'

40. The gap of Glenshane (march)

An Orangemen's marching tune

'That tune used to be played by the Orangemen. It's a good old fife tune. In the old days they had all fife and drums, before the accordions came in, because the old Orange flute was their emblem, and also the Lambeg drum. And it's a very nice tune. I don't know if they would still play it.

The Gap of Glenshane (or Glenshane Pass, to give it its proper title) is on the main road from Belfast to Derry and lies between Maghera and Dungiven in County Derry. I learned the tune years ago in Manchester from a young fella who played the whistle. His name was Philip Dawson, and he came from around Toome in County Antrim. He used to play in the pubs with my brother-in-law, Patrick Keeney.'

41. The Fernden polka

'That's an old tune that was danced at home in the old days. Polkas weren't danced a lot. But there were a few used to dance them around our area, like Pat Harvey, Maggie Keeney, me mother, Ann Diver, and just a few that never would believe in the present. They lived away in the past, because the polka is a very old dance. And in fact the polka is not a British Isles dance at all, it comes from Poland.'

Highlands

'Highlands were danced in different parts of Donegal, and a lot of highlands were danced in Tyrone, strange enough, and then you'd go into Derry, which is just as near to Donegal as Tyrone is, and you'd never hear of them.

It's not the same as the highland schottische, which is very dainty—put out the feet and take them back: the highland is a rough dance, an "eejit's dance"! They're not all that much different from the "flings" they play down south, and in the west country. A fling is even more crazy than a highland. A fling is where a certain group of people decide to go mad, and a fling's a good excuse for turning into a lunatic.

Highlands were played mainly on fiddles, and sometimes melodeons. They are lovely fiddle tunes. They have that fiddle lilt to them. They're pretty good on flutes too. You can't of course play it like a fiddler would, but you can get a good enough highland on a whistle or a flute. But they are really fiddle tunes—they fit the fiddle much better I think.

The reels haven't stories, and nor have the highlands. A lot of the highlands you know never had names, because the highlands were any tune—any reel that didn't make the grade was played as a highland! Highlands were, and they still are, failed reels, and they're hellish nice tunes! The reels were slowed down to fit the dance, and that's when the dance became highlands. A highland is quicker than a strathspey—in between a strathspey and a reel. If you want to make a reel into a highland, you chop it in the middle, because the dance had only one "A" and one "B". Therefore you can play any reel for a highland and any highland for a reel if you speed it up and double it.'

42. Piddling Peggy

Derived from the slip jig composed by Packie (no. 29)

This tune works well as a reel also. On the fiddle, played at a good clip in the key of A, it never fails to capture people's attention.

43. A Gweedore highland

"A real good highland, that'un."

Packie feels that this tune originated in Gweedore (Gaoth Dobhair[30]—the Irish-speaking area of Donegal); nevertheless, it was being played all over the county when he was young.

---

30. Irish *gaoth*, wind, and *dobhair*, foul, wicked.

44. The forgotten highland

"That's an old one—from my cradle days I suppose maybe."

When we visited Packie Manus in 1994, he told us that he had stopped playing the whistle altogether. As a ruse to get him playing, Jean asked Packie to try a wooden whistle he had brought from Canada. Packie promptly played this beautiful tune, which we had not heard before.

> 'That has happened. People'll hand me a whistle and say, "Try that", and while you wait, I'll think of a tune that I hadn't thought of for maybe sixty years.
>
> Names: I have no names for any highlands in fact, because we just got up and danced the thing, and we never bothered the names of the tunes at all. Nobody ever wrote down a tune, and where was the point in somebody writing it, nobody could read it so.'

45. Mín a'Churráin

A traditional highland, of which Packie made an air and march (**Mín na hÉireann**, no. 37)

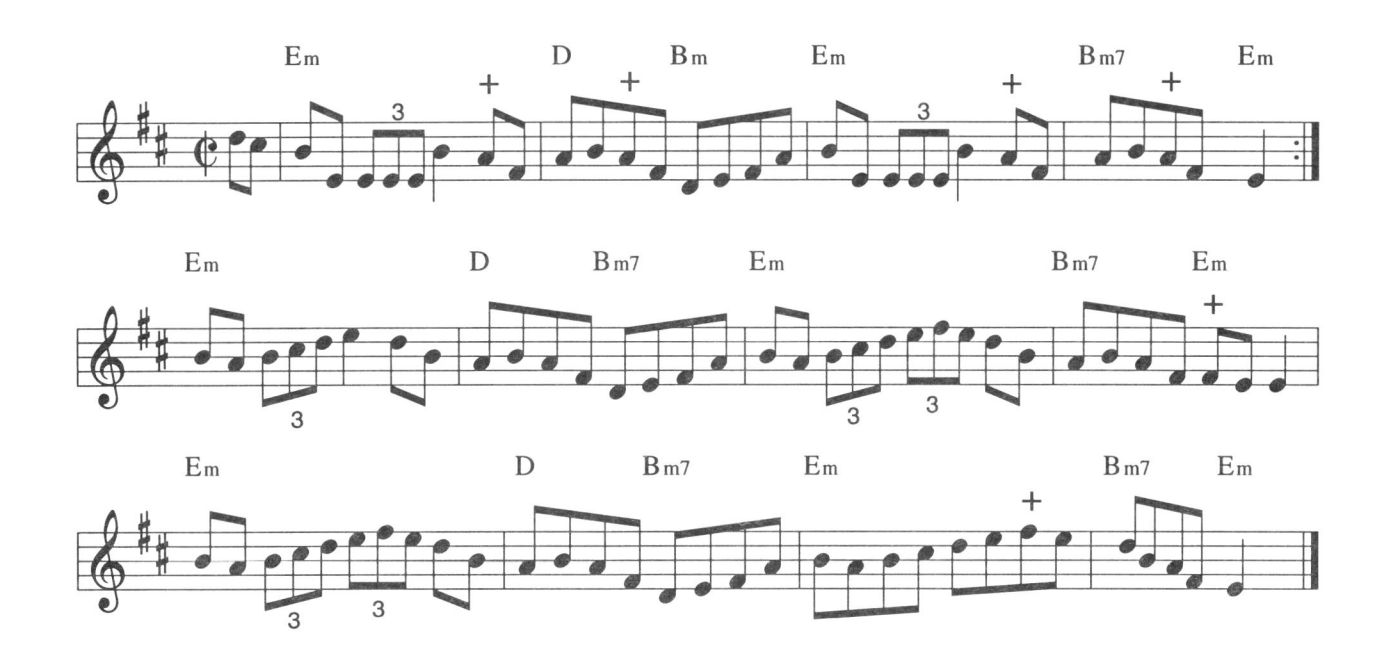

Close to the strathspey *Miss Drummond of Perth* (Athole Collection, p. 260).

Photo: Stephen Jones.

46. The crow's claw (Johnny Haughey's highland)

'That was one of John Haughey's, and my brother-in-law Patrick Keeney used to play it too.

We had the sappers already[31]: before the land was squared, people were disputing about townlands and where Meenbug ended and where Meenadreen started, and all that. If there wasn't a river, the sappers came round. They were from the government. They planted stones and they cut out a sign—crow's feet, two acute angles joined. Sapper's marks, they called them.'

---

31. See no. 12.

47. Welcome home Rosie

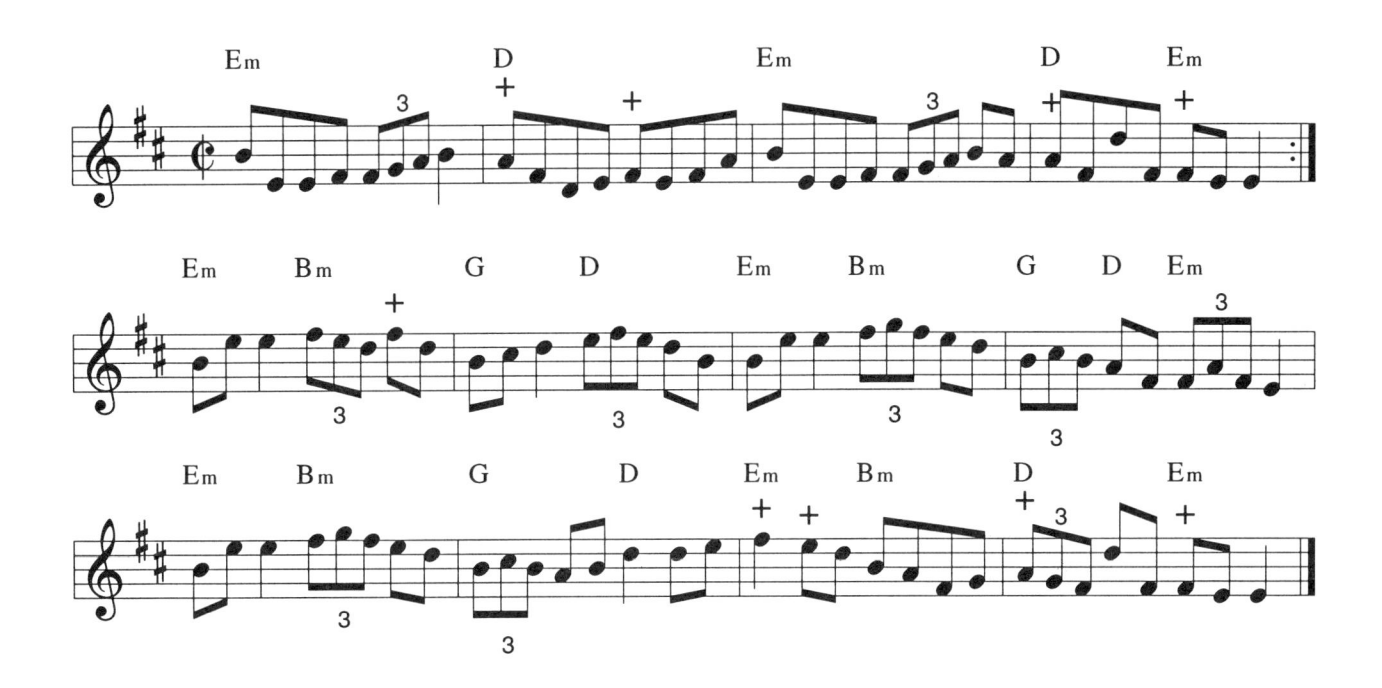

'Welcome home Rosie! I can remember that... Rosie O'Boyle came home from America. She was some relation, as far as I know, of Thomas and John Boyle. She had a real gramophone, they called them in those days. It was a wind-up one, now, all right, but it was really a posh one, and everybody was welcoming Rosie home because she had this marvellous outfit with her. That tune was on one of her 78s.

There was another Rosie that brought a record player back from America. I think she was Rosie Harkin; she's long dead now. She called it a "Victrola". You had to crank it, and put in a new needle every time. She had quite a lot of nice records. We used to call in to her when we were kids at school, because there was no records at all in this area, and she brought this record player from America, and it was the greatest thing. Even the old people used to go in to hear this fellow singing in New York.

And the records were so scraped and battered... She used to stand there, and when it wound down, she would wind it up, and the tune would get back up to speed. Then of course, we would sing it ourselves, trying to imitate the wobbly, screechy sound of the record. She was happy, the poor thing, and she used to make tea for us then.'

48. An fharraige chiúin (The calm sea)

'I suppose it was called that because it was a very tame kind of a tune. That's what it was called. Everybody played it: my brother-in-law played it, and the Gallagher brothers played it.'

This tune is clearly related to the Scottish strathspey *King George IV*, versions of which are played by many Donegal fiddlers, including James Byrne and the late brothers, Mickey and Francie Byrne. When we pointed this out to Packie, he observed that "You'd get no tune from our area named after kings, or queens!"

We have included two playings of the tune to show Packie's characteristic use of melodic variation.

49. An highland fada (The long highland)

'Very Scottish. That's a kind of Scottish strathspey speeded slightly, a Scottish pipe tune.'

The first part of this tune is reminiscent of the reel *The gravel walk to Grainne*. Packie's rendition of this piece is a *tour de force* of whistle playing, demonstrating his tonguing ability and highly inventive variations.

Stephen Jones, Packie Manus and Jean Duval on the Owentocker River bridge, Ardara, July 1994. Photo: Stephen Jones.

50. The last star

'I remember that one played often and often. And it is also Scottish, it's a schottische. It's even played yet in Scotland. They used to put two swords on the floor, and they would dance between the swords. It was then taken over to Donegal and played as a highland, which is about twice as fast as a schottische. My father might have brought that back, he possibly did, maybe. He would be lilting it, and everybody would say, "Ah Daddy for God's sake give it a rest!" (Blaspheming was not reckoned as a sin about our area, and it's not yet, here.) If there was somebody he didn't like, many a time he would say, "I wish he would step on the handle and cut the feet off himself!"

Now, in our area there were several outstanding dancers; there was Pat Harvey, he used to come to our house often, and Hughie Diver. They could dance all night and not give up—they could start at seven o'clock in the evening and dance till twelve, and not get off the floor. And the same musician would sit there for the five hours, no stop. If there was a wee drop of poteen or whiskey, he would pluck the strings with his left hand while he took a drink, keep the rattle going. And the people waiting for him would be tapping out the time. It was a serious thing, when I was a kid, dancing was a big thing. If you weren't a dancer or a singer or a musician, you weren't really welcome at parties you know. If you were just somebody who would go in and sit there and couldn't play or sing or dance, no-one took a blind bit notice of ye, and it's possible maybe you wouldn't get any of the booze when it would come around: they would pass you by because they didn't notice ye at all.

At weddings the dancing would last a long time. Start about two o'clock in the afternoon and carry on all day, all night; and somebody would go home and look after the animals and come back again and it still went on. Aye—summer or winter you never left a wedding in the dark; y'always waited for daylight, even at Christmas, you waited for the sun to rise. It was dancing on all the time. We'll call it *The last star*, because if there was a star in the sky, nobody would go home. "Ah, it's still night, what the hell, Charley!" It was half-past six in the morning![32]'

Two playings of this tune have been transcribed in order to show Packie's use of variation.

---

32. As mentioned in the Introduction, Packie enjoyed the process of finding titles for the unnamed tunes. Having come up with this name, he was moved to comment, "Somebody's going to say, talk about a shower of ____ [lunatics] that wrote this book!"

51. *An t-altán buí* (The yellow-faced rock)

'That's an Irish highland, maybe Donegal, or maybe Tyrone, or Fermanagh: around Lough Erne they used to dance highlands.

An t-altán buí. I'm sure that's what Johnny Haughey used to call it. It's the face of a rock, a yellow rock, which is most unusual, because rocks are grey in our area.'

The first part of the tune displays an obvious kinship with the *Sleepy Maggie–Seán sa cheo–Loch Kyle Castle* family of tunes.

52. We're having a drop

'It's a highland, and a Donegal tune too, played all around here. Tommy Keeney used to play it, and Paddy Boyle would have played it.

Dancing was mainly in the country houses, but later there were some little dance halls. Well now, we used to call them barn lofts, because the barn would be two storeys high, and the top storey would be for dancing on, and sometimes when the building was very old, the floor used to collapse down on cattle below or something. They were all farmer's places. That's where they were all held, in barn lofts, because there was no other place. A lot of the country houses were only small; any that was big enough passed for a hall, of course. When all the furniture was cleared out there was quite a bit of space. Everything was cleared out of the barn loft, and that's where the dancing was held. The neighbours would gather. There was no admission; if there was booze, there would be a little collection. A box went round, or somebody was at the door and said, "We're having a drop tonight," and you knew what that meant.

I remember the floor collapsing at the house of the Gallaghers—no relation, not my Gallaghers—who lived about three or four miles from me. They let the people in and in till there was so many in the floor wasn't fit to hold them up and they went down. There was nobody hurt.'

53. Behind the ditch in the garden

'Big Pat used to play that, surely. It was one of his special highlands. He had a great opinion of himself playing the fiddle you know, he was no ordinary fiddle player. He had to analyse the tune and get the whole ins and outs of it first in his mind before he would play it in company. Very often he used to take the fiddle out and sit, he called it "behind the ditch"—it was a fence between the house and the road, where the old laneway goes into his house. Before the ditch or the hedge there was a very nice little garden in there. So Pat used to sit in there and it was the most sickening thing in the world to listen to—he would play little bits of the tune over and over, and shape it to the way he thought it should be played, and he was usually right you know. He played it out there because the family wouldn't have him in the house, behind the ditch in the garden. There's a nice title for it. And you saw the place today! There's a little laneway with trees on either side, that's where the well was, that's where we used to carry the water from. When I was twelve or thirteen, I remember Pat playing there.'

Once again, two playings of this highland are given to show how Packie typically develops the tune.

54. Lilting Ann

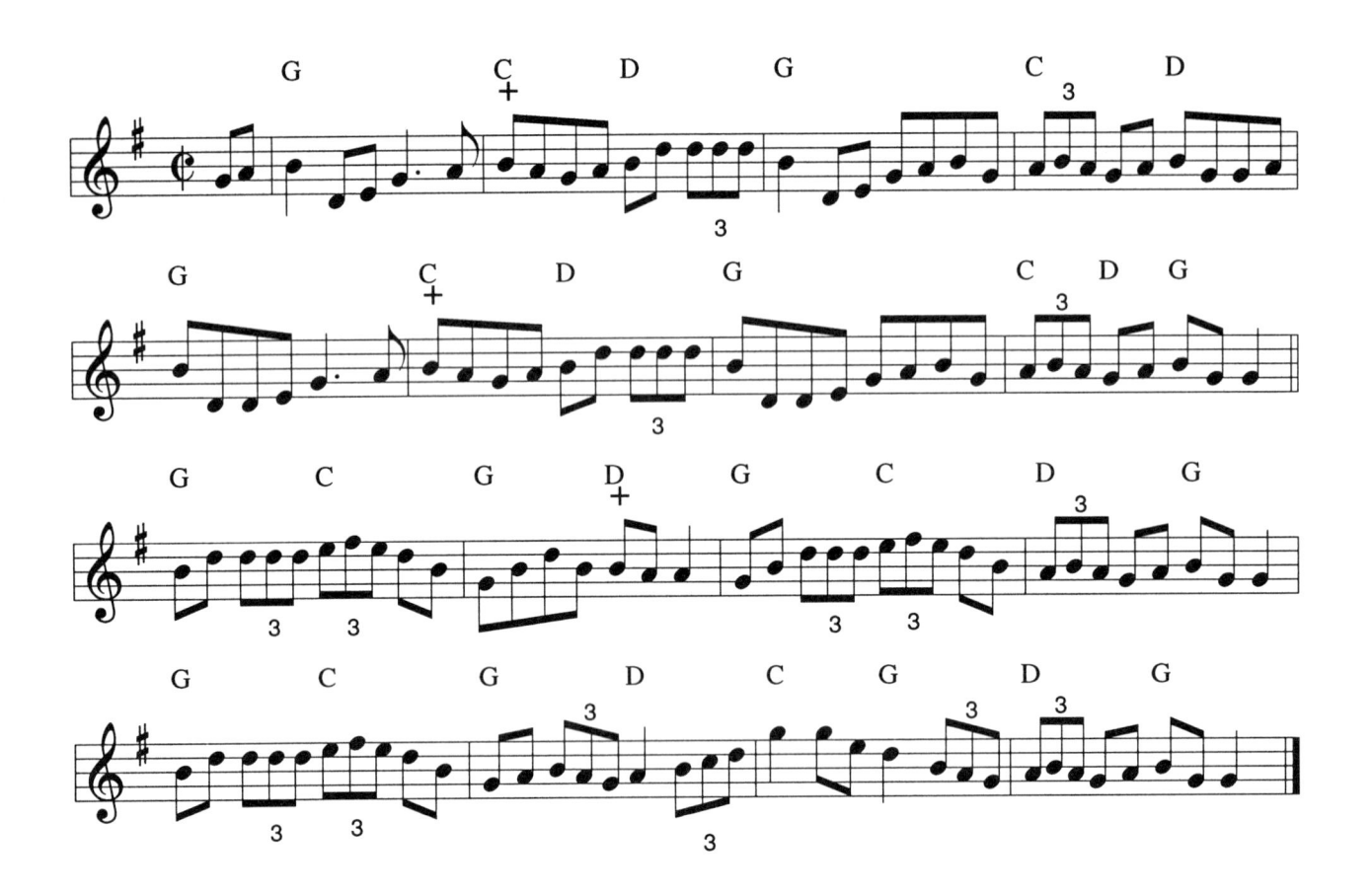

Packie invariably plays this tune with no. 53, **Behind the ditch in the garden.**

'Pat's sister Ann used to lilt that. I don't know if Pat really joined them two together; maybe I did, because playing Pat's tune reminded me of old Ann Byrne. She never married. She was a lovely old character, she was innocent and she was nice going. She wouldn't say a bad word about anybody. Well, neither would Pat, till he would get annoyed, you know; Pat was a really nice fellow till he would lose his temper. She died when I was away to England. She lived in the house with Pat.

She used to walk with a waddle, she was a fairly heavy-built woman. She always lost a note because she had to stop to breathe. Ah, they were happy, the creatures; they had nothing, but they were as happy as could be.

Lilting was the in thing in our area. There were quite a few fiddle players, but they would be away playing cards or something, and when we would be holding a dance, somebody would lilt. Ann Byrne would lilt, or Biddy Sweeney.'

55. Unnamed highland

'That's a popular one. That's being played even yet, at sessions. I can't think of a name for it.'

This tune appears to be a first cousin of the strathspey *Ca' Hawkie through the water* (Athole Collection p. 54), and perhaps a second cousin (once removed?) of the reel *Castle Kelly*.

56. The Willighan bush

'That was a really nice highland, and it sounds Scottish, but it's Irish. We were talking about Pat Kennedy from Dunkineely—that was a favourite tune of his. It's a popular tune all over the west of Ireland.

There was a fellow lived at Meenawillighan. He was John Hilly, and he used to lilt that tune. He had no power to his voice, you would hardly hear him, and he would wave his arm, so that people would see that he was still lilting. He was a lovely singer, and so was his sister. People used to stand between him and the fire in case he would stagger into the open hearth. He was only young but he was feeble.'

This tune is close to the strathspey *Lady Anne Hope* (Skye Collection p. 95, Athole Collection p. 157). An Irish version has been recorded as *Frank Roche's favourite* by the Chieftains and by Matt Molloy. Once again, Packie's turn is quite different.

57. Weans in skirts

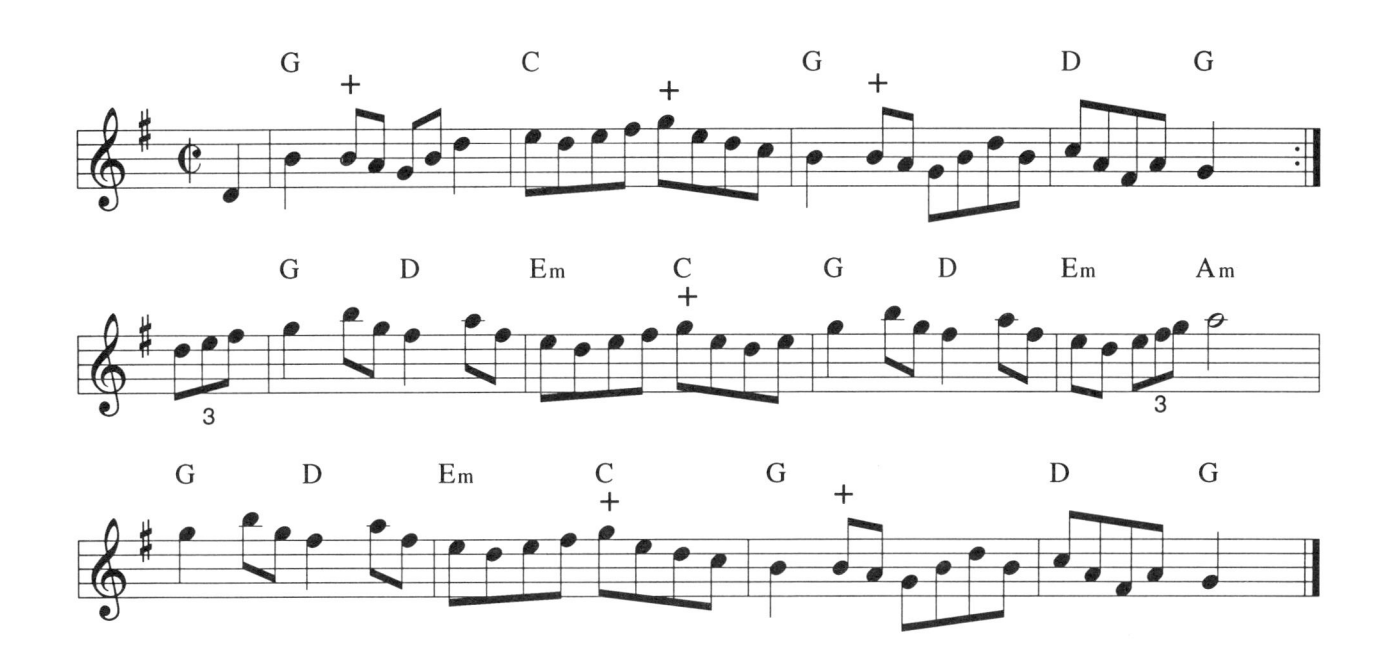

'When we were kids we were called weans—very Scottish. In Derry to this very day they call the youngsters weans[33]. Oh, we were called weans till we went to school. And do you know that we used to wear skirts—not at school though!'

---

33. People in the north of Ireland generally understand the word "wean" (which is pronounced "wane") to be a contraction of "wee ane" (wee one), although some dictionaries suggest as a possible alternative etymology that it is a shortened form of "weanling".

Reels

'The only thing about reels is, you have to be very fit to dance the bloody things; that's the only comment I have to make about them. I never was really into the reels. Every session you go to, it's one reel after another. I remember being at sessions and you wouldn't hear a thing only reels, it would be a full night of reels. I get sick listening to them. I like a jig or a highland or a set dance or something mixed in. [Players today] go to extremes.'

Packie outside Nancy's bar, Ardara, 1985. Photo: Keith Wincoll.

58. The dark girl dressed in blue

An Appalachian tune? Or an Irish one?

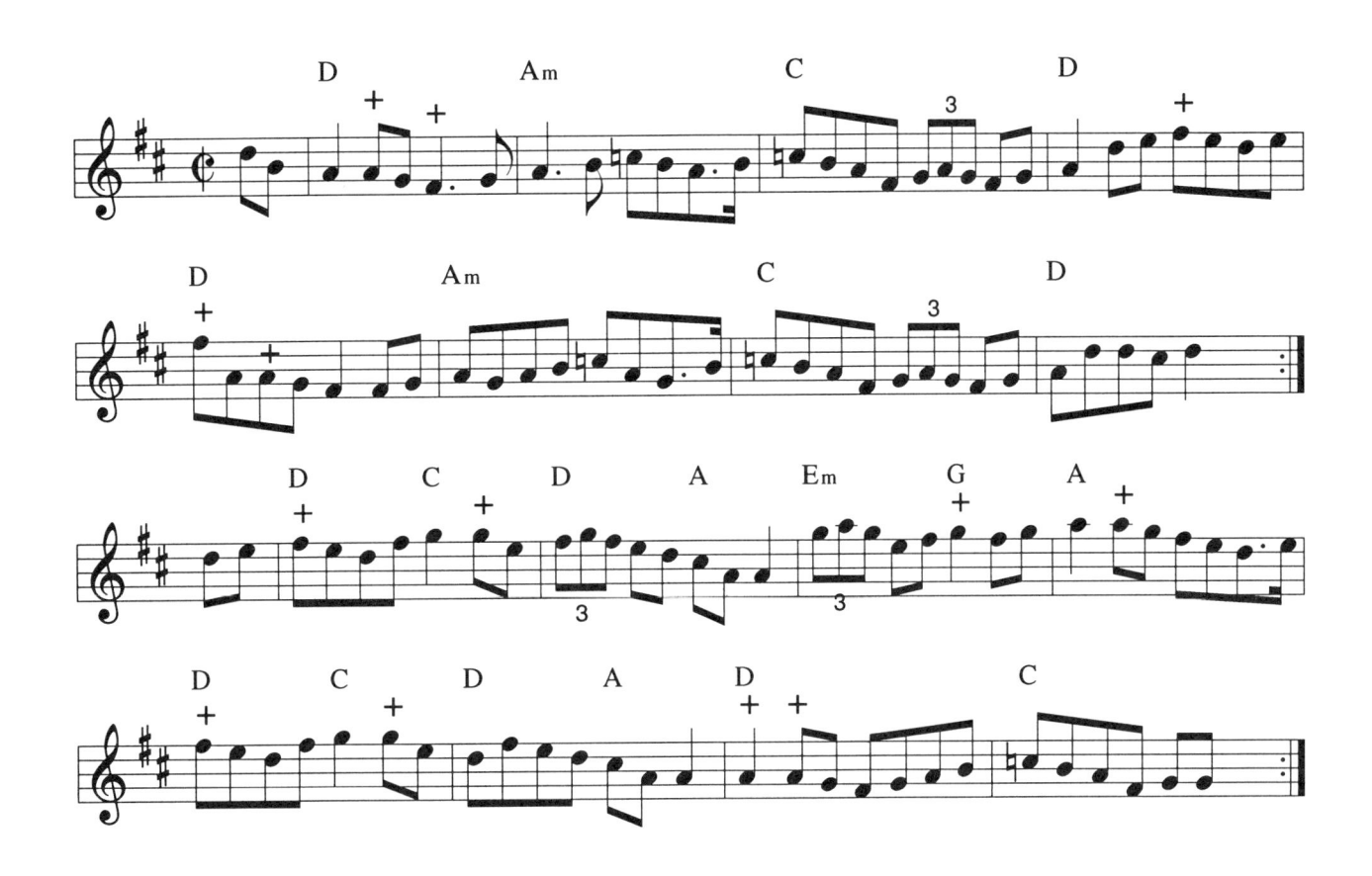

In the notes to the jig version of this tune (no. 4), Packie points out that it came to Corkermore from America in the form of a song tune, and that he made it into a jig. His comments below, however, indicate that it was being played as a reel at house dances in his young days. Many years later, Packie heard the tune played at folk festivals in Britain by visiting American musicians.

> 'That's an Appalachian tune. There was a girl used to be at the festivals in England, she was from North Carolina and she used to do this rag-doll dancing. That was the exact same air she used for a rag-doll dance. Her husband is a storyteller, and her daughter is now at the rag-doll dancing and the storytelling.
>
> It was maybe an Irish tune before it went to the Appalachians. It used to be played for a reel, and they always played it for the very finish of the set, when they would all hold hands, and tap-dance their way out. I made a jig of it, and I made a slow air of it, I was experimenting how many I could do with it, and you could do nearly anything with it, it was very flexible.'

59. The ghost's welcome

A fine tune, and a fine story to go with it

Packie learned this fascinating tune from his grand-uncle Big Pat Byrne. Here is the gist of the story that invariably accompanied Pat's playing of the tune:[34]

> One night, while Pat was on his way home from a wedding or ceili in the early hours of the morning, he took shelter from a sudden storm in an abandoned house. As his eyes adjusted to the dark interior, he realized that there was another man in the room. They began to converse and when Pat learned that the stranger was a fiddle player, he suggested they pass the time by playing tunes. The other man promptly played this unknown tune, which immediately mesmerised Pat. They played on, but the stranger mysteriously vanished as the first light of dawn appeared in the window. Pat, realizing the stranger was a ghost, named the tune.

---

34. The story is told in Pat's words in **Recollections of a Donegal Man**, pp. 85–87.

'Pat played it that way, and every time he played it he told the story. Pat had a very good memory, he could tell the story exactly the same way, and maybe he would tell it two or three times for one evening.

The house in the story belonged to Rosie McHugh.[35] She lived away on the hill facing Corkermore, and when she died in the house, it was supposed that there was a ghost there, some man… You know the way that people talked years ago: if a woman was carrying on with a man or vice versa, something bad was surely going to happen to them. It appears there was this fellow hanging around with Rosie, and nobody liked him because he was playing around with her. When she died there was a curse put on him and he became a ghost in Rosie's house. Do you know that Big Pat believed those stories.'

Packie recorded this piece on THE HALF DOOR, an album that is well worth hunting out for his playing of this tune alone.

---

35. See **Rosie's brachán**, no. 73.

60. Call the horse!

A Packie Manus composition

'Every animal about the house was a pet, and there was a good few of them. Sheep and cattle and ponies and donkeys. If my father got his way and if he had land enough, he would have plenty animals strolling about, and it was my job to look after them. On dairy farms every cow has a name, but we never gave names to animals. But we had one very big red horse I remember, and he was Paddy. And if he was way on the top of Meenadreen, which was across the river, he used to wander on the roads and wander up people's lanes and go into people's gardens and eat people's corn. He could look after himself. Somebody would come out of our house, which would be over a half mile from where he would be, and shout "Paddy!" and he started for home. He knew he was wanted, there was work to be done, aye. At night you couldn't see him, he would more than likely be eating somebody's corn. My father would say, "Call the horse." And I would go out and shout "Paddy!" You would listen then for a while and the next thing you would hear was the flop! flop! flop! He was coming towards you at his ease, coming home to go into the stable for the night. Oh, he used to come home every time. And I remember when my mother used to call him, and she had a kind of a sharp voice, he knew her voice too. And strange enough then if one of the neighbours called him he wouldn't take a blind bit notice of them.'

Photo: Stephen Jones.

61. Blow the bellows

A Packie Manus composition

'At one time, straight across the river here [in Ardara], the Byrnes had their forges there, when you turn out the Donegal road from the Diamond, it's the first building on the right. When I would be coming into the town, Saturdays mostly, I used to be sent into the town to do shopping, and I would spend an hour or two in the forge listening to the boys, telling lies. The blacksmith James Byrne himself was a little fat man, and he would talk continually. He would put the iron into the fire, and he would be doing something else but he was still telling the ould yarn, you see. He would take out the iron and he would get the hammer and give it a beating, but he never missed a word of the story.

They were a rare lot. The blacksmith was the only man that worked. The rest of them used to sit in that forge, or go home for their grub and come back and sit in the forge again, telling lies. 'Twas lovely and warm in there in the wintertime! There was one fella, Paddy Seán, and you'd go in there in the month of July or August, and Paddy would be right in beside the hearth with a big—we used to call them fisherman's overcoats—heavy overcoat on, buttoned up to his neck. He used to have the coat on so tight in case a breeze got at him, and he would have a big safety pin in it, and it was so tight up round his throat that he couldn't turn round. He used to sit on an iron box, and if anybody came in, he would swivel round, like a swivel chair! He could stick that, not a dew of sweat on him, and you know what a blacksmith's fire is like when it's going. He was used to it! He was there all his life.'

62. An coileán cú

A Packie Manus composition

'That's Gaelic for a hound pup, a young hound. There's a story about that. This fellow—now how did it go that he became the owner of *a coileán cú*—somebody was going away to England or America and gave him a wee pup. He kept the pup and he thought it was the greatest thing in the world and he was feeding it and looking after it until one morning he couldn't find his socks. So he went out to the yard in his bare feet and there were his socks torn to pieces. So he just came in and caught the pup and choked him. That's the *coileán cú*.

I don't know where the story came from or who the man was, but there was a fellow lived beyond the river used to tell it, Pat Ban. There were two Pat Hegartys: Black Pat and White Pat. This one was Pat Ban and the other was Pat Dubh. They were from Meenadreen, straight across the river from us. I've no idea what age I would be when I made the tune up, but I wasn't very old, I can tell you that, because Pat is dead a long time. He died shortly after Big Pat, so I would have been seventeen or eighteen I suppose when he died.'

Photo: Stephen Jones.

63. An bata tí (The house stick)

Reel or highland?

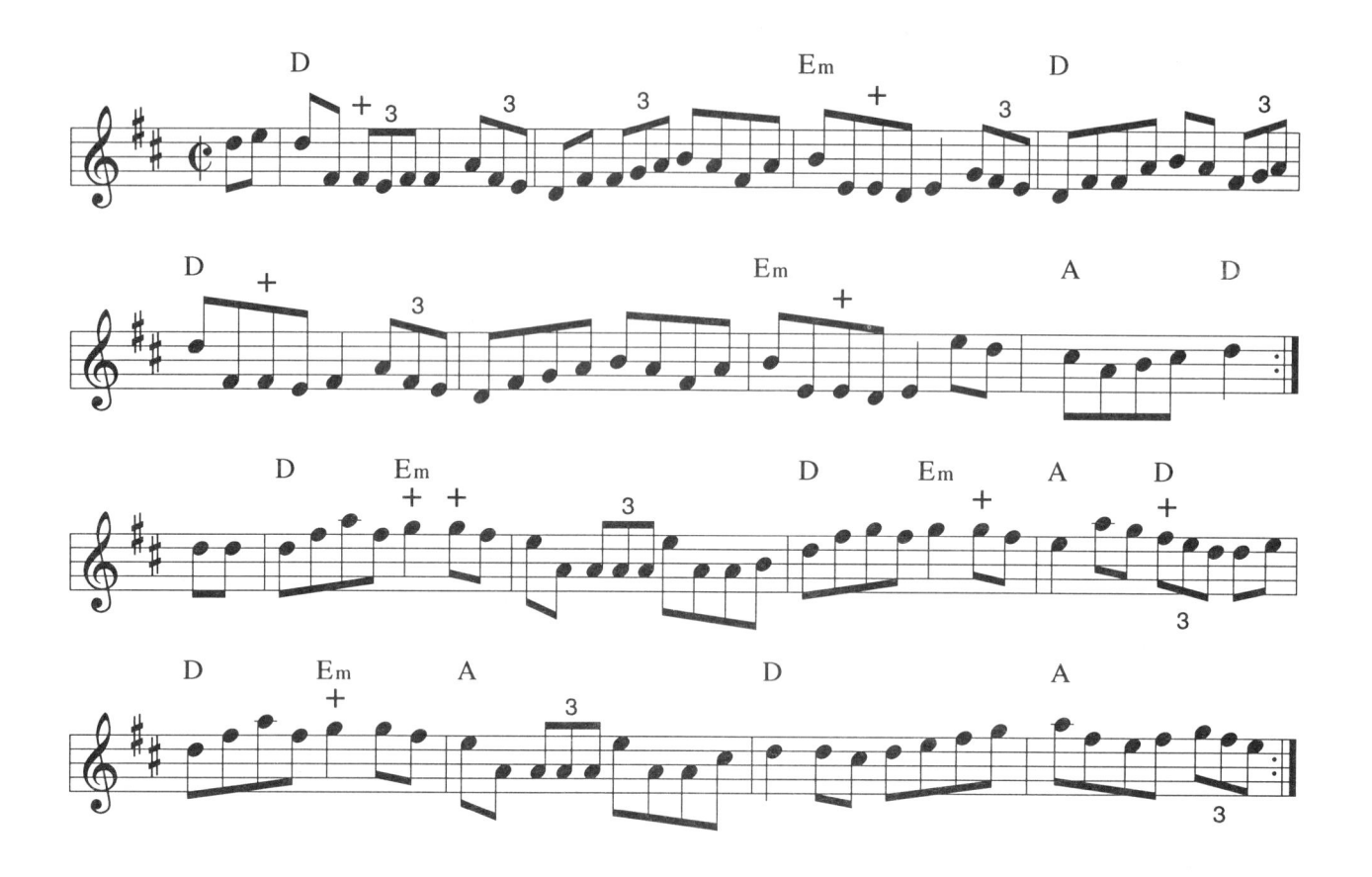

Packie feels that this tune works equally well as a reel or as a highland. The name emerged after we noted a family resemblance between the tune and the well-known reel *The blackthorn stick*. The house stick was a long piece of bog timber that formed the main beam, or couple, of the roof of a house.

> 'I've no idea of the age of it, because when you hear something when you're a youngster, you don't take much notice of what age it was. But seventy-five years ago, they were still old tunes at that time.'

The tune is similar to one recorded by Cape Breton fiddler Howie Macdonald on THE dANCE lAST NiGHT as *Sullivan's Strathspey*.

64. The three stars

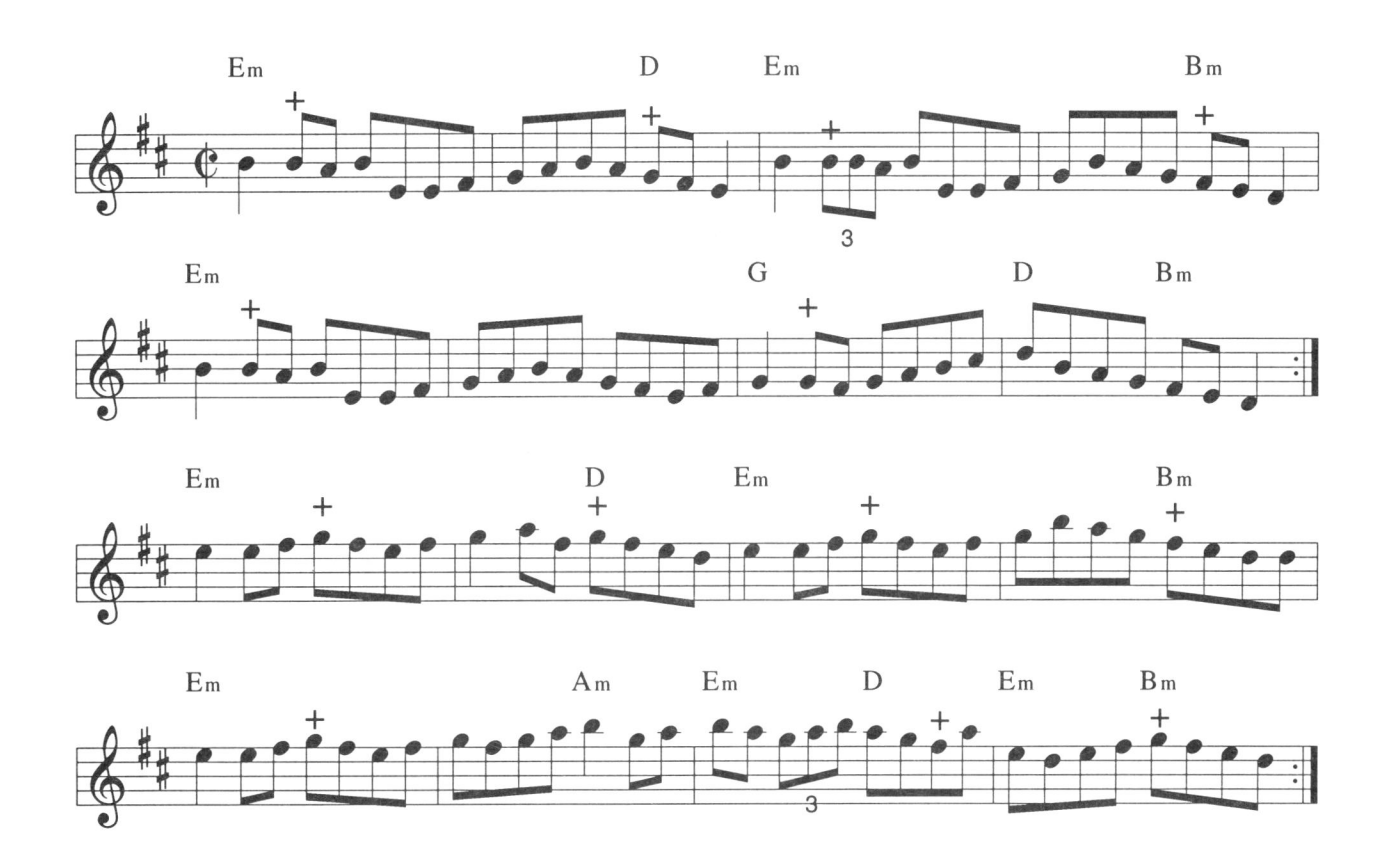

Jean christened this otherwise unnamed reel: during an early review of the transcriptions, Steve, liking the tune, had pencilled three stars on the sheet. Packie felt this was an apt name, reminiscent of another Donegal reel (not to mention a play by Chekhov), *The three sisters*.

Hornpipes and germans

'I don't know how the name "hornpipe" came about. I reckon maybe that because the hornpipes are old tunes, maybe they were played on horn pipes. They used to say, the reel was the up-and-down one, the jig was the round-and-round one, and the hornpipe was whatever you wanted to make of it! You could dance a hornpipe fast or slow, to reel time, or to very slow time.

They would be solos, or face to face, but no contact. In the german and the highland, you have contact, arms around each other, but not in the hornpipes. I saw in **Riverdance**, they linked arms in a hornpipe, and I wonder who thought of that, because that was never known of. I have never seen that, but I have seen no end of hornpipes danced by couples and groups of up to ten or twelve.

We used to dance germans to hornpipes, because that was what we knew best. We would probably have to lilt them as we were dancing.

Barn dances and germans: I don't think there is a difference, and another thing, I don't know why they were called barn dances. A barn dance is a heap of people gathered in a barn loft. That was a barn dance as far as I was concerned. In parts of America they used to have hooleys in barns, and it was a great go around here. We called them germans, and I don't even know how they were called germans, because there's nothing at all German about them! It's possible maybe that someone called it a German barn dance, and then they cut it down, they called it a german, and that stuck. That was a very popular dance, for as many couples as could get on the floor. 'Twas face to face couples, just like a highland.'

65. Unnamed german

An American german!

'I think that is a corruption of an American dance. I don't know why I got that notion about it, but I did. We used it as a german. And I remember it as a hornpipe. I've only heard it played around Donegal here. I can't remember hearing it anywhere else. I don't have a name for it, but the thing about it is, German dances did not have titles.'

This is a setting of a very widely known tune, an English version of which is known as *The Durham rangers*. The American tune Packie refers to is possibly *John Brown's body*.

66. The Bonnie hop (german)

A particularly attractive and sprightly tune

'I remember us putting that on an LP (THE HALF DOOR). Bonnie used to like playing that one. It's rather nice. I haven't the foggiest where it came from. I don't have a name for it. *The Bonnie hop?* Well really, that'll do it grand—Bonnie loved it!'

Packie and Bonnie Shaljean played together as a duo for more than 10 years from the mid-1970s. Audiences loved them, not only for their magical music, but also for their unpredictable stage rapport. Here they appear to be having a difference of opinion about tuning! Photo: Bob Naylor.

67. The stuttering auctioneer (hornpipe)

A traditional hornpipe, with a third part added by Packie

'That was a hornpipe from some time ago. It would be a good enough tune for a german, too. The third part is mine. We'll call it something stupid, like *The stuttering auctioneer*. Did you ever hear of an auctioneer stuttering? Because they can talk like hell. G-g-going, g-going, g-g-g-g-g-gone!'

68. The tatty hokers (hornpipe)

A Packie tune with a distinct Scottish flavour

Alternative first line

'I used to like that tune, you know. It's a bit cheerful, it's not one of these dreary, dragged-out things. It sounds like one that I might have made up? Well, I did! It's one of the very few that I made up that I like. It's a Packie tune all right. I tell everyone it's Scottish, because I think it sounds a wee bit Scottish.

"Tatty hokers" was a name given to the men and women, the seasonal workers, who would go over to Scotland in the autumn and gather potatoes. Hoking means taking something up out of the ground, like if you're pulling weeds, you're hoking. People from this area used to go over to Scotland every year. Walk from here to Derry first, and then go on the cattle boats to Ardrossen.

I remember a couple of years ago, I was very bad with arthritis, the two legs got beat up on me, but Jimmy McBride was running one of his weekend sessions of traditional singing, so of course he invited me along, and nothing would do Packie McGinley[36] only I would go. Between the broom and the walking stick, he got me into the car, and we landed down in Buncrana, at Jimmy's do. I had to be helped out of the car and into the pub. This fella, I thought I had never seen him before, but he was staring at me. He was a big fella, and I started getting a bit afraid, and I thought, this man has some spite to me, because he won't take his eyes off me.

We went out then for a meal, and Jimmy says, "Would you believe this, there's a man in there that knew you long years ago. You travelled on a boat with him from Derry to Ardrossen, and you had a boatload of cattle with you." That was Charlie McGonagle. They were all singing on the boat, and nobody knew me. So when I thought the singing was beginning to die down—of course it was something like nine hours on a cattle boat at that time from Derry to Ardrossen—I said, "Is it all right if I give a song?" So I sang about twenty songs for them then, and Charlie was only a young lad, just after leaving school, and he was going to tatty hoking, and he still remembered me. "The last time I saw you," he said, "you didn't need any sticks." I was carrying one, though, but that was for cattle.

To this very day they have tatty hokers in Scotland. But there's nobody going over now from Donegal to tatty hoke. They go to do other things, like the hydroelectric schemes. And they don't live in their little bothies away out in the wilds no more. They all have flats!'

---

36. Packie Manus' friend and neighbour in Ardara.

69. Barefoot Biddy (hornpipe)

A hornpipe lilted by Packie's neighbour, Biddy Sweeney

'Biddy Sweeney was a small woman who never wore shoes. She had shoes, because she would carry them with her, till she would come to the wood there and then put them on to go into Mass, and come out again and take them off. She could not get along with shoes, she wasn't brought up with them. And she could walk through whin fields and on the sharp stones of a road.

She was extremely intelligent—as bright as could be. She used to love lilting for us, and to watch us dancing. She was a good dancer herself, and a fluent Irish speaker. She would lilt loud, you could hear Biddy very plain away outside in the yard.'

70. The schoolmaster's sister

A slow hornpipe composed by Packie

'That's a tune of mine. It puts me in mind of the sister of the schoolmaster, Susan McDyer. She used to play slow hornpipes on a squeezebox out in the school yard, and we used to march to them, and sort of dance to them, when we were toddlers, when we were weans.'

Packie plays this tune at ♩ = 105.

Mazurkas and waltzes

'Mazurkas have gone out of fashion, and the tunes for the mazurka won't fit any other dance. And the Varsovianna is the same: it went out of fashion, and the tune for it won't fit any other dance. So the tunes died with the dances. Although it is still done: when they had the Wednesday night dances down here at Peter Oliver's[37], mazurkas were very popular. And *Shoe the donkey*, that was another one that used to be danced regular down there. But only around here. I've never seen them anywhere else.

The trouble is, you see, to dance anything like *Shoe the donkey*, or the barn dance, or the highland, they're really meant to be tapped out, like Varsovianna and all the other ones. But nowadays, there's nobody tap-dancing. I see them dancing highlands and they're sliding along on a polished floor. Their feet never leave the floor, and they call that a highland.

For the mazurka, you'd play just the one tune, and you'd play it maybe up to ten times. There would be tapping, but it wouldn't be really loud, you know it would be kind of mild tapping. Because even mild tapping would be thought nowadays as wild, 'twould be a stone breaker now. A man dancing with hobnailed boots on a flagged floor, he's going to make some racket you know, so he'd have to cool it down as much as possible. The women used to have little horseshoes on the heels of their shoes specially for tap-dancing.

Taking them all round, you know, there were maybe ten mazurkas. Only around here, and in about Kilcar and Gleann Cholm Cille, and Donegal town, where they took up this set dancing thing, they included mazurkas. But they're never seen anywhere else, even in the Irish scene in Dublin, or London, you'd never see it. Too strenuous!

Waltzes: these "old-time" waltzes weren't danced. Believe it or not, they only called them old-time waltzes to go crazy. We used to dance what we called "modern waltzes", nice and slow. The English dance bands used to play them in the mid 40s and 50s. They changed them around here, speeded them up. You couldn't keep up with them.

Yes, a slip jig played fast can sound like a waltz too, but I don't know should they be mixed because they're two entirely different dances, and they're different tunes, and they should be treated differently. In fact some waltzes, I know how they should be treated. They should be all painstakingly written down and then burned!'

---

37. Peter Oliver McNeilis, former proprietor of The Central Bar in Ardara.

71. Father Murphy's topcoat (Shoe the donkey)

> 'Where's the point in putting that in the book? Anyone that ever picked up an instrument played *Shoe the donkey*, because it's a simple as falling off a log.'

Despite Packie's comment, we decided to include this tune: even if every musician in Donegal knows it, we are sure there are many further afield that do not, just as there are many that do not know the dance...

> 'Once we were coming home from Miltown Malbay, Packie McGinley and me, and we stopped in at a dance festival in Sligo, and they were doing their best to dance this *Shoe the donkey*, and they hadn't a great idea of how to do it. We were sitting about, anyway, and taking no notice, and this girl came in with cups of tea to us. So I said, "Oh, I see you're shoeing donkeys around here." She says, "Ah, that bloody thing's going on all day, and they don't seem to be coming much speed with it"—they were only young kids. There was a woman teaching, and I asked, "Would she mind if I...?" "Oh, she says, come on," and she got the cup out of me hand. So she dragged me out anyway, and we had a whale of a time. I showed them how to do *Shoe the donkey*, and they were quite pleased about it.'

A different setting of this tune appears in THE ROCHE COLLECTION as *Father Halpin's topcoat*.

72. Alla Pío

A tune, supposedly Mexican, from Packie's jazz-band days

This piece came from a reel-to-reel tape of tunes that Packie himself recorded in 1969. He is puzzled by our wish to include it in the collection. While there's no denying that it is an oddity, and while we think it unlikely to prove a huge hit with readers, it is a little reminder of Packie's varied musical history.

> 'It's a Mexican tune, more in waltz time than fandango time. It's a picture of **Father Murphy's topcoat**, only it changes away then. No, I didn't decide to make *Shoe the donkey* into a Mexican dance! I learned that when I was playing saxophone in dance bands right after the war.'

73. Rosie's *brachán* (mazurka)

'I don't know if that was the real name for that tune. It was a made-up kind of a name. Rosie was noted for her *brachán* (porridge): she could make the best porridge of anyone in our parish, so that's how the name came about. The Rosie was Rosie McHugh.'

74. Home from France
(Sa bhaile ó'n Fhrainc)

'I think that was an English song away back in the old days. The Irish might be only semi-educated in the old days, but they had brains. If they heard an English song with a lovely air to it, like this, they put Gaelic words to it to make it Irish.'

Photo: Stephen Jones.

75. Unnamed mazurka 1

This tune and the following one are well enough known inside and outside Donegal, but we think players will appreciate Packie's settings of them.

76. Unnamed mazurka 2

Photo: Stephen Jones.

77. The dangers of men

The air to a song composed by Packie Manus

The air to a witty ditty Packie wrote for his friend, the singer Julie McNamara. Not wishing to pre-empt a recorded version of the song that is in the pipeline, we have not given the text here.

Airs

'I'm very fond of the airs. If I was younger and had the same enthusiasm about airs that I do now, I would do a study of the Irish airs, because 'twould be a very interesting thing. They all had songs to them. Very few reels or jigs have any songs to them, but all the airs were belonging to songs, and that is interesting in itself, to wonder, what kind of a song was attached to this, or what kind of an eejit composed the words...'

As mentioned in the introduction, the number of airs given in this collection does not do justice to Packie's fondness for these too-often neglected representatives of the Irish musical tradition.

Packie Manus at the head of Glengesh Pass, West Donegal, August 1987.
Photo: Stephen Jones.

78. Suan cloch teineadh
(The firestone lullaby)

A version of this tune, but lacking a second part, is used as the theme music of GLENROE, an RTE television program. [38]

---

38. Given in Ó Canainn, TRADITIONAL SLOW AIRS of Ireland, no. 81, as the Glenroe theme.

'Only the first eight or nine notes resemble the "Glenroe theme" music. The rest of the air is entirely on its own and a bit obscure. I have never heard words to it. There is no indication that the witch or fairy mother in the story[39] was using words. 'Twould be worth giving some thought to it.

The *cloch teineadh* was the friendly part of the house: if a neighbour came in, they were always put as near the *cloch teineadh*, as near the hearth as possible. It was a stone just set in the floor. In the old days people never wore shoes in the house, they were always in the bare feet, and the floor was earthen, made of what they called "till"—hard, packed soil. All the cooking for cattle, poultry, people and all, was done on one fire, and naturally when you're doing a lot of boiling, you'll have sparks of water coming out of the pot. And the sparks of water coming down on this very hard-baked till made it like ice, and youngsters racing over and back in front of the fire could slip and fall into the fire. To counteract that they put down a big freestone, or whinstone, flag in front of the fire. No sooner the water hit this hot stone than it dried up, and there was no danger.

Then there was another stone attached to the fire, but it was leaned against the wall, and there was a space that left a kind of a tunnel behind this stone. And that was for crickets: the crickets brought in good luck, and they were nice and warm in there. You'd be sitting at night, and as soon as the light would go, these crickets would be chirping like hell, singing away. And then the little so-and-so's ate the toes out of your socks!'

The tune was played by Big Pat, and here is the story he told about it:

> Long, long ago at the foot of the Blue Stack mountains there lived a young shepherd and his wife. They had one little baby girl, four months old, but the poor little thing was very weak and ill. 'Twas plain to see that she wasn't meant for this world, but the loving parents did everything they could to make her short while on earth as comfortable as possible. Her mother watched her day and night and her father made for her a wickerwork cradle from willow rods that grew down by the riverside. Now, in those days the mountain people believed that if a baby became ill it sometimes meant that the fairies had taken away the real baby and left a sickly one, known as a "changeling", in its place. But we shall see farther on whether that was so in this case.

---

39. The story that Big Pat told to accompany the tune, reproduced below.

The first heavy snows of the winter usually came around the middle of January and that was when the shepherd and his dogs had to keep a watchful eye on the sheep, which were moved down to the lowlands to keep them safe from snowdrifts and avalanches. This particular shepherd didn't have many sheep of his own, so he took responsibility for the ones belonging to his neighbours in that area. He was very knowledgeable and honest, so the other sheep owners knew that their flocks were safe under his supervision. They gave him every assistance and help they could offer, but in spite of that he was having a term of bad luck which no-one could explain: his sheep were dying without any apparent reason. He found his two best dogs dead on the same morning and now his baby wasn't likely to live very much longer. Only for the love, comfort and encouragement of his wife, he would have given up.

The sky became heavy and dark grey in colour, and the winds, holding a southwesterly arc, whistled and moaned around the cottage. All the signs of a snowstorm descended on the mountain, so 'twas time to move the sheep on to more level and sheltered land. The shepherd and his wife were up early. He fed his only remaining dog, a very old grey collie called Vance. His wife made up a *kelkin*,[40] which means a bundle of food wrapped in a large handkerchief, and off he went to the mountain. It snowed all day and by evening there was a fairly deep fall.

The baby was in her rod cradle on the firestone. Her mother heated some milk to feed her but when she lifted her, she found her dead. Just then a knock came at the door, and when the shepherd's wife opened it she saw the outline of a woman with a baby in her arms standing in the dark night, her clothes and hair covered with snow.

"God bless you," said the woman. "My baby is hungry. Could I ask you for a little milk?" "You can, and welcome," said the shepherd's wife. "I've just heated some for my own baby but found her dead when I picked her up."

"Do not cry for her," said the woman. "The good people will provide for you for the rest of your life."

When her baby had the milk taken the woman picked her up, wrapped her woollen cover around her and walked into the night, humming a tune. By this time the shepherd was returning home, having settled the sheep in a safe area. He heard the most beautiful female voice. He had no idea where it was coming from—he couldn't see owing to the darkness. But the voice was there, humming what seemed to him an enchanting lullaby, and being a musician he understood its beauty. The voice seemed to be heading for the river, so under its spell he followed after until it died away in the snow-covered rocks above the water. He turned towards home, but the lullaby and the sound of that voice were the only things in his mind. He came into the house and sat down without removing his coat or hat, completely ignoring his wife, who was sitting at the fire, crying and holding the dead baby to her breast.

---

40. Possibly *cuilcín* in Irish, related to *cúilín*, a crust of bread.

He was lost in the magic of the lullaby, and strange to relate he could memorise every note exactly as the voice had sung it. He kept humming it over and over till at last he took his fiddle down from the wall and started playing. His fiddle had never sounded so nice before, and he had never played so well or with such confidence. He was in a world of his own, hopelessly lost in the lullaby and the sound of his own music. A sense of peace and happiness seemed to come over him, together with a feeling of joy and contentment. For him, time stood still and nothing was moving, until suddenly his wife's scream brought him back to earth and lifted him out of his fantasy. He looked towards her, and there was their baby, red cheeks and blue eyes, smiling and wriggling on her mother's knee, very much alive and well.

That baby grew up to be a very beautiful girl and a brilliant musician, playing in the great halls and castles of royalty and the rich. Renowned for her beauty, she had offers of marriage from lords, earls, dukes and noblemen, who showered gold and jewels on her, but never married. She stayed close to her parents and was with them at their very end. She often played the lullaby that had brought her back to life, and dedicated it to her father, the poor shepherd, who taught it to her. No, she was no fairy child, no changeling; she was very much a shepherd's daughter who owed her existence to her kind mother, who gave a simple cup of milk to a hungry baby, and to her father, whose music brought her back from death.[41]

---

41. Packie believes that this tale was a way of reinforcing the idea in people's minds that if you do someone a good turn, you will get a good return. This version was written out by Packie for possible inclusion in a book of stories. A slightly different rendition appears in **Recollections of a Donegal Man**, pp. 77–78. There, Packie concludes by saying, "Legend has it that the strange woman was really a fairy mother who paid the shepherd's wife for her kindness by returning her baby and taking away the changeling."

79. An bothán (The little turf house)

The air to a song heard once

'The Irish name of that is *An bothán*, which means a little sod house. There is a Scottish song with that air to it that I only heard once in my life from a fellow that used to work in Scotland during the tatty-hoker period. When he'd come back, he would always circulate a few of the tunes that he picked up. I can't remember anything about the song, but it was called *The shieling*, which is really much the same as a *bothán*. I always liked it, and I played it for years.

All those words means the same thing, really, which is a shelter: in English, *bothán* became bothy, and in Ireland a *bothóg* or *bóitheach* was a shelter for animals, say for sheep at lambing time.'

80. The true lovers' discussion

The air to a song sung by Packie's mother

The song sung by his mother had, according to Packie, thirty-one verses of eight lines each!

'I can't remember all the songs my mother sang. We all ran when she'd start singing this one. I remember my father saying, "That's not a song, that's an endurance test!" He preferred comic songs, but she hadn't much time for comedy. There's another song to the same air: *The maid of sliabh na mBan*. It's from Tipperary, or Cork, or somewhere down that way.'

81. The barley field (air and hornpipe)

A well-known dance tune skilfully transformed into an air

'I changed the timing of the dance tune, which of course was a german or a hornpipe, and I put the air before it using the same notes, but with the timing all changed.'

We include Packie's playing of the well-known hornpipe for no better reason than we like what he does with it.

The roundtower at Bruckless Church, the church attended by Packie Manus and his parents.
Photo: Sharon Creasey.

82. The spinning wheel

The original air to a well-known song

This tune, according to Packie, is the original air to the song made popular by Delia Murphy.

> Mellow the moonlight to shine is beginning
> Close by the window, young Eileen sat spinning
> Bent o'er the fire, her old grandmother sitting
> A-droning and crooning and drowsily knitting

'That was the old original air for *The spinning wheel*. Delia Murphy was going somewhere to do a concert and she forgot her music, and *The spinning wheel* was in it. And the fella that was driving her said, "Ah, stop worrying, we'll make an air for it." And by the time they got to the venue, they had the air that is now used for the song. But the old air: my mother, and lots of people, used to sing that. She used to do it to the timing of the footboard of her spinning wheel.

This was one song that my father liked to join in on. He always said, "Whoever composed that song deserved new socks and a clean shirt for every Sunday in the year!"'

83. The Glen Finn lass

A song widely circulated in the old days

The song *Finn waterside* appears as no. 240 in SONGS OF THE PEOPLE: THE SAM HENRY COLLECTION.[42] We are grateful to John Moulden for providing us with the words.

As I roved out one evening, being in the summer time
I heard a voice made me rejoice, to wait I did incline
I overheard my own true love, so sweet as he did sing
"Come down along Finn waterside," he made the woods to ring

My parents thought all in my prime for to banish me away
To dwell among the Indians and leave sweet Inver Bay
But I'll let them know before I go, whatever may betide
That I have a true love of my own, dwells nigh Finn waterside

There is many a clever tall young man lives nigh Finn waterside
But above them all, both great and small, I would rather be his bride
I would rather hear my own true love sing in the month of May
Than all the herring fish or ling that swim round Inver Bay

Farewell unto Finn waterside, where oftimes I have been
Likewise unto sweet Inver Bay, adieu, you woods so green
You lofty mountains I must cross, they do call Barnesmore
Down by the rocks and yon rural well and along by the salt sea shore

---

42. SONGS OF THE PEOPLE (ISBN 0 8203 1258 4): edited by Gale Huntington and Lani Herrman with contributions from John Moulden. University of Georgia Press.

84. A Welsh chapel hymn

'I never knew any of the words to the hymn, because it was always sung in Welsh, and I don't know a word of the Welsh language. It's very like a hymn sung in the choir at home, *Never will I sin again*.

To this day I cannot figure out how these tunes and songs came into a remote area like here. Today it would be different because you would have people moving from one country to another, but in those days nobody went anywhere only to Scotland or America. Nobody went into England and definitely nobody went into Wales! But, apparently the tunes got here, some way or other…'

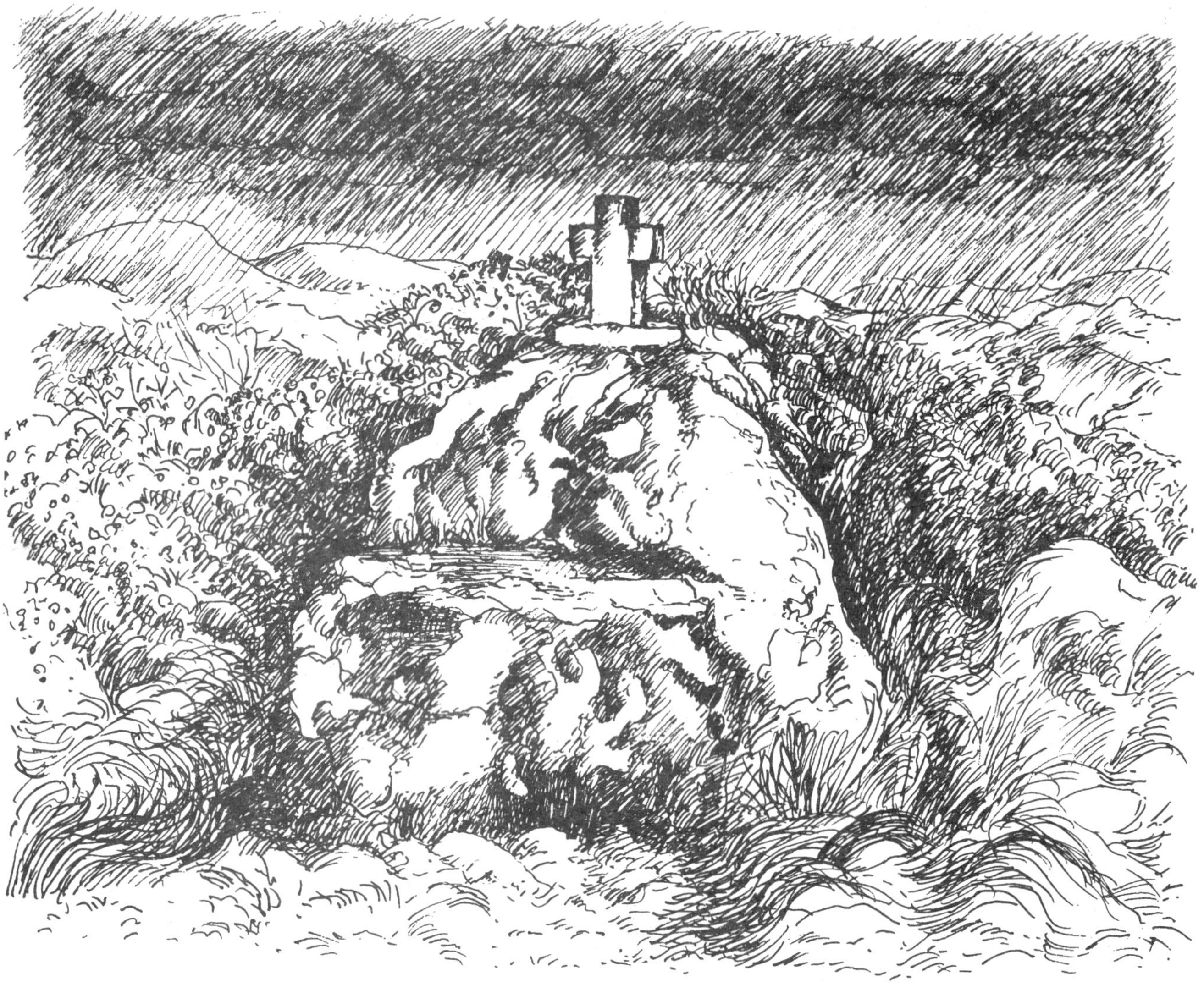

85. Ar thaobh na Carraige
(By the side of the rock)

This is the air to a song Packie heard sung in Irish by Tommy Sweeney, brother of "Barefoot Biddy" Sweeney. It is an entirely different air to that of the well-known song admired and popularized by Seán Ó Riada, *An raibh tu ar an gCarraig?*

> 'My versions of some of these tunes were not really heard like Seán Ó Riada's version, and therefore people would say, "That's not it!" They may be right, but who knows whether that was it or not? There's no such thing as perfection in traditional music!'

In the editors' opinion, this is an outstandingly beautiful air, and provides a worthy finale to this remarkable body of music.

Index

A
Alla Pio	128
Ar thaobh na Carraige	149
Away and over	51

B
Barefoot Biddy	124
Barley field, the	142
Bata tí, an	116
Behind the ditch in the garden	100
Belling march, the	76
Besom of heather, the	75
Blow the bellows	112
Bonnie hop, the	120
Bothán, an	140
Buckasheen landy, the	62
By the side of the rock	149
Byrnes of Gleann Cholm Cille, the	36

C
Cailín rua, an	67
Call the horse!	110
Calm sea, the	92
Captain Taylor's march	80
Coileán cú, an	114
Collier laddie, the	64
Crossing the Oily river	38
Crow's claw, the	90

D
Dangers of men, the	134
Dark girl dressed in blue, the	32
Dark girl dressed in blue, the (reel)	107
Dawn pack, the	70
Dossan of heather, a	40

F
Father Murphy's topcoat	127
Fear dall, an	61
Fernden polka, the	84
Fharraige chiúin, an	92
Firestone lullaby, the	136
Forgetting the lesson	26
Forgotten highland, the	88
Foyne's legacy	50
Fumbling chorister, the	74

G
Gap of Glenshane, the	83
Ghost's welcome, the	108
Glen Finn lass, the	146
Gweedore highland, a	87

H
Half door, the	58
Highland *fada*, an	94
Home from France	130
House stick, the	116
Humours of whiskey	71

I
I'll marry you when me garden grows	52
I've got a bonnet	78

J
Johnny Haughey's highland	90

L
Last star, the	96
Lazy wife, the	46
Lilting Ann	102
Little turf house, the	140
Long highland, the	94

M
McShane's rambles	28
Merry hours of gladness	37
Mín na hÉireann	79
Mín a'Churráin	89

P

Paddy Bhillí *na rópaí*	65
Peeler and the goat, the	53
Piddling Peggy (highland)	86
Piddling Peggy (slip jig)	68

R

Red-haired girl, the	67
Rosie's *brachán*	129

S

Sa bhaile ó'n Fhrainc	130
Sapper, the	45
Schoolmaster's sister, the	125
Sheigh o' rye, the	44
Shoe the donkey	127
Showers of autumn	48
Socks on the crane	54
Spinning wheel, the	145
Stepping stones	34
Storm, the	30
Stuttering auctioneer, the	121
Suan cloch teineadh	136
Swamp reed march, the	82

T

T-altán buí, an	98
T-éan sa chrann, an	60
Tatty hokers, the	122
Teelin rowdies	42
Three stars, the	117
True lovers' discussion, the	141
Tummel march, the	73

U

Unnamed mazurka 1	132
Unnamed mazurka 2	133
Unnamed highland	103
Unnamed german	119

W

We're having a drop	99
Weans in skirts	105
Welcome home Rosie	91
Welsh chapel hymn, a	147
Wheels of the train, the	56
Willie dear	47
Willighan bush, the	104

Y

Yellow-faced rock, the	98